24 GREAT walks in VENICE

WILEY

Wiley Publishing, Inc.

Author: Philip Curnow
Managing Editor: Apostrophe S Limited
Series Editor: Donna Wood
Page layout: Andrew Milne
Copy Editor: Hilary Weston
Proofreader: Stephanie Smith
Picture Researcher: Luped Picture Research
Production: Stephanie Allen
Image retouching and internal repro: Michael Moody

Edited, designed and produced by AA Publishing.
© Automobile Association Developments Limited 2009

Published in the United States by
Wiley Publishing, Inc.
111 River Street, Hoboken, NJ 07030

Find us online at Frommers.com

Frommer's is a registered trademark of Arthur Frommer.
Used under license.

Cartography provided by the Mapping Services
Department of AA Publishing

Map Data © New Holland Publishing (South Africa) (Pty)
Ltd. 2006

A03625

ISBN 978-0-4704-5370-4

A CIP catalogue record for this book is available from
the British Library.

The contents of this publication are believed correct
at the time of printing. Nevertheless, the publishers
cannot accept responsibility for errors or omissions,
or for changes in details given in this guide or for
the consequences of any reliance on the information
provided by the same. Assessments of attractions and
so forth are based upon the author's own experience
and, therefore, descriptions given in this guide necessarily
contain an element of subjective opinion which may not
reflect the publishers' opinion or dictate a reader's own
experiences on another occasion.

Colour reproduction by Keene Group, Andover
Printed in China by Leo Paper Group

OPPOSITE: LOOKING ACROSS THE LAGOON TO SAN GIORGIO MAGGIORE

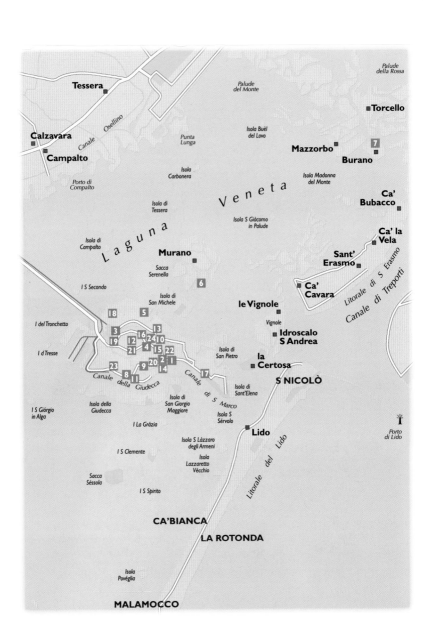

CONTENTS

Introduction

Which Venice would you like to experience? The colourful city of gondolas, carnival and mass tourism, or the feisty city that fought great battles and defeated determined enemies to become the greatest economic and political power in the Mediterranean? This phenomenal Republic developed over a course of nearly a millennia, from the 7th century to its demise at the end of the 18th century.

The walks in this guide take in the whole Venetian experience, allowing you to explore the alleys, quays, filled-in canals and squares, from the wide-open spaces of the Public Gardens in the Castello district to the narrowest passageways well off the beaten tourist track. They lead you to places where ordinary Venetians such as fishermen, boat builders, traders and artisans lived and worked during the time of the Republic.

There are approximately nine types of thoroughfare in Venice: The 'calle' is the most common, a long narrow path between buildings; 'salizzada' is a larger path, which was the first to be paved; 'ramo' is a small street which offered access to a main passageway; and 'ruga' is similar to a 'ramo' but flanked by shops and houses. As for the canals, a 'rio' is a small transit route which would be closed at night, a 'rio terà' is a filled-in, now pedestrianized version and a 'piscina' is literally the last of the lagoon ponds or pools to be filled in. A 'fondamenta' or 'riva' runs along the canals and gives the waterside dwellings extra stability. As for the squares, typical of all Italian towns and cities, there is only one: the famous Piazza San Marco or St Mark's Square. All the other open spaces are called 'campo'. Do be aware that the local Venetian authorities have made their signs in Venetian dialect. Most official Venice maps, and the maps in this book, are, however, in Italian.

To get around the city keep the Grand Canal as a reference point and use the vaporetti or waterbuses to move from one part to another to begin or end your day. For a stay of three days or more the most economical way to do this is to purchase a Venice Card. This card combines unlimited vaporetto travel as well as entry into the city's principal churches and museums, although entrance to St Mark's Basilica and other specific sites such as the

Peggy Guggenheim Collection require an additional fee. For stays of less than three days Tourist Travel Cards are available, although church and museum entrance is not included.

For first-time visitors to the city with only a few days to spare the classic obligatory walks take in Rialto (Walk 4), the Grand Canal (Walk 3) and Palazzo Ducale (Walk 2). If you can, also try following in the footsteps of Marco Polo (Walk 10).

As you walk around this magnificent floating city, look beyond Casanova, masked balls and the period of the Grand Tour when public show, theatre and excess seemed to have become daily life. Try to discover its true splendour and energy, and rediscover the time when Venice looked outwards and succeeded in making this small corner of the Adriatic Sea a place to live and prosper against all odds.

WHERE TO EAT
€	=	Inexpensive
€€	=	Moderate
€€€	=	Expensive

The Merchants of Venice

An easy walk from the quay at the Palazzo Ducale to the Old Arsenal, where commercial galleys and military galleons were constructed.

It took seven hundred years for Venice to grow from a huddle of lagoon islands frequented by fishermen into the strongest military and commercial power in the western world. It then took another six hundred years of intrigue, formidable battles and myopia for the Republic to lose almost everything it had. It seems that the city was a victim of its own success. The noble patrician families lost interest in the sea and the trade that had made them powerful, and became complacent. Some Venetians say this happened when the Republic turned down a trading partnership offered by the King of Portugal for the new spice route around Cape of Good Hope. From then on the markets of Hungary, Germany and France took their business elsewhere. This walk links the two elements of the Republic that made it great: the political heart of the city near Piazza San Marco and the Arsenal where Venetian ships and galleys were built in secrecy.

From the entrance of Palazzo Dandolo, now the luxury Hotel Danieli, cross over the Ponte del Vin and step onto the quayside, the Riva degli Schiavoni.

Throughout its history, the Schiavoni race were the Republic's most loyal servants. The name refers to their origins in Slavonia or Dalmatia, present-day Croatia. Riva degli Schiavoni means 'quay of the Schiavoni' and at this prestigious spot near the Palazzo Ducale the clan would moor their boats and unload. Right to the very end of the Venetian Republic the Schiavoni demonstrated their dedication and courage many times. When the end finally came in 1797 a solemn ceremony was held in Dalmatia, during which this tough race openly cried.

2 Leave Riva degli Schiavoni by turning away from Canale di San Marco and entering Calle del Vin, immediately on the left after the Ponte del Vin. As Calle del Vin widens into Campiello del Vin, keep right until you reach Salizzada S. Provolo. Make a right turn, then keep straight on for Campo San Zaccaria.

The church of San Zaccaria dates from the 9th century. It was here that the Italian word *broglio* found common use as a meaning for electoral fraud or general corrupt scam. (Perhaps not Venice's most refined cultural gift, but the word is 100 per cent Venetian.) It derives from *brolio*, the tree-lined passageways that once marked the porticoes flanking Piazza San Marco. They stretched all the way

to the church of San Zaccaria and they offered shade for covert meetings and the purchasing of favours. Do visit the crypt that remains flooded for most of the year.

3 Leave Campo San Zaccaria by backtracking along Salizzada S. Provolo. Take the first right into Campo

WHERE TO EAT

[O] OSTERIA OLIVA NERA,
Castello 3417, Salizada dei Greci;
Tel: 041 522 2170.
Fine traditional Venetian cuisine, including fish soups, duck and the famous deep-fried floured courgette flowers of the house. €€

[O] TRATTORIA AI CORAZZIERI,
Castello 3839, near Campo Bandiera e Moro;
Tel: 041 528 9859.
This family-run trattoria is in a tranquil corner off the tourist track where Venetians carry on their daily business. €€

[O] AL COVO,
Castello 3968, Campiello de la Peschiera;
Tel: 041 522 3812.
Small and intimate restaurant featuring two air-conditioned rooms with comfortable leather chairs. Original paintings by Italian artists adorn the walls. In summer the tables move out on to the small square. No shorts or flip-flops. €€

DISTANCE 1.5 miles (2.4km)

ALLOW 2 hours 30 minutes

START Ponte del Vin before the Hotel Danieli

FINISH Museo Storico Navale (Naval Museum)

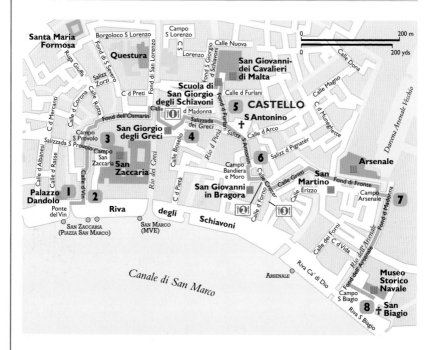

San Provolo. Continue ahead, passing the Ponte dei Carmini on the left, on into Fondamenta dell'Osmarin. A left turn then a first right over the two Ponte de Greci bridges leads into Calle della Madonna.

The church of San Giorgio degli Greci was the focus of the Greek community that had flooded into Venice following the fall of Byzantium in 1453. Dedicated to St George, the community was allowed to practise Greek Orthodox rites following the construction of the church. The neighbouring Scuola di San Nicola and the Istituto Ellenico di Studi Bizantini house precious icons and liturgical art. Many of the artefacts were saved during the Fourth Crusade in 1204 and now form one of the largest collections of Christian art in the world.

4 From the church of San Giorgio degli Greci, exit the square by Salizzada dei Greci. Look out for the Schola S. Zaccaria – La Commedia dell'

OPPOSITE: THE ELEGANT CAMPANILE OF THE CHURCH OF SAN GIORGIO DEGLI GRECI LISTS GENTLY OVER THE CITY

Arte Ritrovate on the right, which is located in a one-time butcher's shop. The stone-carved 'Salumeria' (delicatessen) sign is still visible along the top of the shop window. Cross the bridge over the Rio della Pietà canal and turn left into Fondamenta Furlani until the Scuola di San Giorgio degli Schiavoni looms into sight to the right of Ponte de la Comenda.

Dating from 1551, the Scuola di San Giorgio degli Schiavoni is protected by three saints, one of whom is St George. On the outside of the building, canal side, there is a frieze depicting the saint killing the dragon in classic pose. Inside is the famous cycle of paintings by Carpaccio, including *Scenes from the Life of Saint George*. A special act protected the paintings from being removed. To the right of the Scuola di San Giorgio degli Schiavoni is the church of the Cavaliers of Malta. The building dates from the 11th century, when it belonged to the Order of the Knights Templar.

5 Backtrack along Fondamenta Furlani into Campo San Antonino where the church of San Antonino is located. Keep right and continue along Salizzada S. Antonin, which opens into Campo Bandiera e Moro on the right. On the left side of the Campo is the 8th-century church of San Giovanni

in Bragora, where composer Antonio Vilvadi (1678–1741) was baptized.

Today's Campo Bandiera e Moro was the scene of a tragicomic incident in 1819. During Carnival a circus elephant escaped and ran riot along the Riva degli Schiavone to Campo Bandiera e Moro. The poor beast was unceremoniously bombarded by cannon fire in the square.

6 Exit Campo Bandiera e Moro by the small alley to the immediate right of the church entrance into Calle di Crozer. Don't take Sotoportego dei Preti on the left, but turn into Calle Gritti, second left. After the Ponte Storto, the church of San Martino and Campo Arsenale face the imposing Arsenal.

The church of San Martino dates from 1540, the golden era of Venice. This building was linked to a confraternity of caulkers. The caulkers had one of the most important roles in boat construction, waterproofing the hulls of the galleys. This afforded them a privileged position in Venetian society but at a disastrously high price: if a ship leaked and sank it meant instant expulsion from Venice for the caulker and his family. The original part of the Arsenal area was established by the Doge Falier in 1105, the year a fire devastated Venice, but what we see today dates from the mid-15th century. At its height, the Arsenal was delivering three ships a day. In 1574, in order to demonstrate the incredible efficiency of the system, a galley was completed from scratch

in the time it took royal guest King Henry III of France to enjoy a banquet in his honour. The stone lions standing at the entrance were brought to Venice by Francesco Morosini as war trophies from Piraeus and Delos in 1692. They symbolise the supremacy of Venice over the Adriatic Sea.

7 Leave Campo Arsenale by the new wooden bridge over Rio dell'Arsenale onto Fondamenta della Madonna and then Fondamenta dell'Arsenale. Continue walking towards Canale di San Marco and the Museo Storico Navale in Campo San Biagio, at the water's edge.

The church of San Biagio dates from 1052 and once held services of both Latin and Byzantine rites, confirming Venice's deep cultural links with Constantinople. Nevertheless, it is the adjacent Museo Storico Navale or Naval Museum that more clearly illustrates the practicalities of running a regional superpower. The museum is housed in a former ship's biscuit warehouse. The rations of *pan biscotto* soaked in wine and water kept the galley crews alive and the trade of the Republic afloat. Interestingly, scurvy was unheard of, as the frequent stops in foreign ports allowed a regular diet of fresh fruit and vegetables.

8 Return to Piazza San Marco and the starting point of the walk by following the Riva degli Schiavoni all the way along the Canale di San Marco.

OPPOSITE: ONE OF THE STONE LIONS WHICH ADORNS THE TERRACE OF VENICE'S ARSENALE

Absolute Power of the Serenissima

This walk is a classic journey of discovery, taking in St Mark's Square, the Palazzo Ducale and the Basilica, with a detour to view the Ponte dei Sospiri.

The power of the Republic of Venice, also known as the Serenissima, a word derived from the Italian '*sereno*' meaning 'serene', or most serene in this case, gained real momentum from the early 12th century. From 1109, the Doge's full title was extended to territories beyond the lagoon, but his power in relation to the Italian mainland did not pass beyond present-day Mestre. Yet it was the Fourth Crusade in 1204 that really sealed Venice's position as the most powerful Mediterranean power of the time. The crusade never reached the Holy Land. Venice had agreed to supply the ships for the venture but soon realized it would never recoup its investment. Following Venetian pressure the fleet headed towards Constantinople, where the city was sacked. Many of Venice's mythical symbols were brought to the Republic including the statues of the four bronze horses that adorn St Mark's Basilica. It was also at this time that the famous Maggior Consiglio (Great Council) was established, and the occupation of Crete, or Candia, that lasted 500 years.

1 Enter Piazza San Marco from Calle larga dell'Ascensione, where the information point is situated. The Museo Civico Correr is in the Napoleon wing above, but first head to the opposite corner for a full view of the world-famous piazza.

This civic museum houses a flag used to commemorate the quelling of an uprising against the Doge by a group of nobles in 1310. Giustina Rossi accidentally killed the insurgent's standard-bearer when a large stone block fell from her window frame onto the poor man. The event unnerved the attackers and they dispersed. For her efforts, Giustina's rent was fixed for life and she was allowed to hang a commemorative flag from the window every year on the day the plot was foiled. Subsequent owners kept up the tradition until the end of the Republic in 1797.

2 From either under the portico or just inside Piazza San Marco, follow the Procuratie Vecchie to the Torre dell'Orologio or clock tower.

The clock tower was built as a symbol of the Republic's ability to see distant horizons. It was also the last thing that condemned men ever saw of the Serenissima, as it was in direct eyeline with the two columns between which criminals were traditionally hung, drawn and often quartered. The clock, by Zuan Carlo Ranieri, is a brilliant example of 15th-century engineering. It symbolized that time in Venice was not dictated by

liturgical necessity but by the secular rhythms of commerce, toil and rest.
TORRE DELL'OROLOGIO;
www.museicivicimveneziani.it

3 Leave the clock tower and walk towards the Canale di San Marco. You'll find the entrance to the Basilica di San Marco (St Mark's Basilica) immediately on the left.

The basilica, altered and added to many times over the centuries, was rebuilt in the mid-11th century at the wish of Doge Contarini during a power struggle between the Patriarch of Venice and the Pope. The work was finished in record time (just eight years) and said much about the religiosity of the Serenissima to its people. Unfortunately, though, such was the haste of the reconstruction,

DISTANCE 1 mile (1.6km)

ALLOW 3 hours

START **Museo Civico Correr**

FINISH **Caffè Florian in Piazza San Marco**

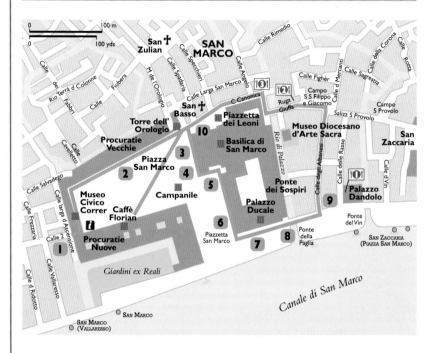

the continuing stability problems of the Basilica date from this period. The body of St Mark has rested in the crypt of the Basilica since 1094, although for many years no one quite knew where. The saint's remains arrived in Venice in the year 828, having been removed from a monastery in Alessandria in Egypt by two merchants, Buono di Malamocco and Rustico di Torcello. To avoid being caught with their prize, they hid the saint at the bottom of a basket containing pork meat. The Muslim guards had no desire

to check the container and sent them on their way.

BASILICA DI SAN MARCO;

www.basilicasanmarco.it

4 Exiting St Mark's Basilica, continue towards the Canale di San Marco and follow the exterior wall to the left.

At Porta della Carta is a striking sculpture of four suspicious characters conspiring with one another. Set in the corner of the building, *I Tetrarchi* is probably a

OPPOSITE: A CUSPIDATE GOTHIC CROWN TOPS THE ORNATE BASILICA SAN MARCO

Syrian work, and it was once thought that the four characters depicted are Moors discussing plans to steal the treasure of St Mark's. The truth is that they are the two Emperors of the west and east Roman Empire of the late 3rd century AD, Diocletian and Maximian (junior emperors), in discussion with their Caesars, Galerius and Costantantius Chlorus.

5 A 180-degree turn reveals the Campanile or bell tower at its imposing best.

It is almost impossible to believe that the fine bell tower we see today, the focal point of the city and an iconic national monument, is only just over 100 years old. On the morning of 14 July 1902, the original tower collapsed suddenly for no obvious reason and had to be completely rebuilt. Amazingly, nobody was killed or even injured as the tower had fallen in on itself, and circumstances led some to

say it was a miracle. First, the gold statue of Archangel Gabriel was found intact, having fallen from the very top of the bell tower where it had stood since 1513. Second, the largest of the tower's bells, the *marangona*, which had been brought to Venice from Constantinople, was also found in one piece and third, most amazingly of all, a Murano glass cup used to celebrate the opening of the original tower was also found intact. Exactly 10 years later to the day, the new bell tower reopened as before.

6 Proceeding from the base of the Campanile, follow Piazza San Marco as it goes on to become the smaller Piazzetta San Marco.

The two famous columns at the end of the Piazzetta have seen it all. Almost every key moment of Venetian history has taken place within shouting distance. Above all, however, this was the spot where capital

punishment was carried out. Everyone from disgraced Doges to common criminals and the Republic's enemies were hung, impaled or beheaded between the two columns. Three columns were originally transported from the Orient, but one was lost overboard in the lagoon. The remaining two lay by the quay for almost a century before being raised in 1172 by a device using wet ropes. As the ropes dried they shortened in length and slowly lifted the huge columns. The inventor was engineer Nicola Starantonio Barattiero from Bergamo, the man who built the first wooden Rialto drawbridge. He was rewarded for his inventiveness by being granted the Republic's only gaming license. The engineer was allowed to run a dice table, but with one condition – it had to be between the two columns (just to keep an eye on him, of course).

7 Looking back towards the bell tower and Piazza San Marco, the entrance to Palazzo Ducale is on the right under the portico.

Within Palazzo Ducale is a clearly indicated circular walking route that takes the visitor through all the main rooms central to the power of the Serenissima. Most impressive is the stunning Sala del Maggior Consigilio, 174x79ft (53x24m) in size with a richly decorated ceiling rising to 33ft (10m). Surprisingly, the room has no columns and was designed to intimidate foreign dignitaries, ambassadors and guests. On one wall is a single painting, *Paradiso* by Tintoretto (1518–84) one of the largest oil paintings

in the world at 75x23ft (23x7m) and the ultimate declaration of Venetian supremacy and confidence. Votes on the constitution and laws were taken in the presence of a thousand of the city's most important nobles beneath this painting.

PALAZZO DUCALE;

www.museicivicineveneziani.it

8 Exit Palazzo Ducale by turning left and stepping onto the Ponte della Paglia for a view of Ponte dei Sospiri, the famous Bridge of Sighs.

The canal separating the main structure of Palazzo Ducale from the prison is called Rio di Palazzo. From here, the Ponte della Paglia offers the best view of the Ponte dei Sospiri (Bridge of Sighs). Ponte della Paglia is named after the straw deposited here, used both for prison cell bedding and as animal feed. This was also the spot where corpses pulled out of the water were left for identification by the crowd. The name 'Bridge of Sighs' refers to the faint voices of the condemned that could be heard by passers-by. The bridge has a two-way path. One section took the prisoners to the cells while the other was for court functionaries. A death sentence required the agreement of eight of the 10 advisors of the Doge. Even if the guilty survived their term in the cells, they would have to pay court costs and for food and lodgings before they were allowed out. Non-payment of these fees meant no freedom and an indefinite stay at the Doge's pleasure.

WALKS IN VENICE;

www.walksinsidevenice.com

9 Having crossed the Ponte della Paglia take the first turning on the left into Calle degli Albanesi. Keep straight on to Salizzada San Provolo and bear left into Campo SS Filippo e Giacomo, which leads into Ruga Giuffa. Cross over the bridge onto Fondamenta de Canonica. Turn left into Calle Canonica, which opens into Piazzetta dei Leoni.

Today, this corner of Piazza San Marco is just a thoroughfare for tourists. It takes its name from the two red marble lions dating from 1722 that guard it. Adjacent Birreria Leoncini, meaning Little Lions, was a favourite drinking spot and meeting place for Fascists prior to World War II. Almost hidden by the massive structure of Basilica San Marco is the church of San Basso, where the funeral of highly regarded sculptor Jacopo Sansovino was held. Having contributed to the arcaded Procuratie Vecchie on the north side of the square, and to many other artistic works during the 16th century, he died in 1570 at the ripe old age of 91.

10 Enter St Mark's Square near the clock tower and cross the piazza towards the famous Caffè Florian, which is under the Procuratie Nuove.

The first recorded mention of coffee in Venice was around 1585, following reports that the coffee bean was being used by the Turks to produce a stimulating beverage that kept men awake. The first specimens to arrive in

WHERE TO EAT

🍽 RESTAURANT TERRAZZA DANIELI,
Hotel Danieli,
Riva degli Schiavoni, 4196;
Tel: 041 522 6480.
The Restaurant Terrazza Danieli occupies the top floor of the Danielino building, one of the palaces that forms the Hotel Danieli. The restaurant serves an à la carte menu of typical Venetian cuisine. €€€

🍽 AL GIARDINETTO,
Castello 4928 near Ruga Giuffa;
Tel: 041 528 5332.
Typical Venetian dishes have been served here for a century. Try the *sarde in soar* (sardines in sweet and sour sauce) and *granceola* (spider crab) with a fine wine. €€

🍽 TRATTORIA LA CANONICA,
San Marco 340, Calle Canonica;
Tel: 041 520 9299.
Typical downtown restaurant with a nice terrace. Look out for the portrait of Casanova. €€

the city were sold as medicine before becoming commercialized right under the portico of the Procuratie, from a stall known as Dell Arabo. By the end of the following century over 30 coffee houses had sprung up serving this fashionable drink in and around Piazza San Marco.
IL CAFFÈ FLORIAN;
www.caffeflorian.com

The Grand Canal on Display

This walk combines a series of short vaporetto hops to discover the Grand Canal, Venice's main street and the central artery of the city.

The Grand Canal is 2.4 miles (3.8km) long and follows the course of an ancient river bed. For centuries, anyone who was anyone in Venice had to have a palace facing the Grand Canal. As the ultimate demonstration of wealth and power the owners cemented their status by giving their names to the palaces. Approximately 200 buildings line both sides of the canal. They stand as a roll-call of Venice's oldest and most important families, whose history parallels that of the city. These families, including Mocenigo, Contarini, Dandolo, Michiel, Falier, Tiepolo, Badoer, Zen, Corner and Morosini, formed the elite of the Maggior Consiglio (members of the exclusive general council). Although many had alternative accommodation within the city, the canalside palaces were more than just luxurious homes. They became offices or function rooms and were even rented out to the Serenissima to host royalty and high-ranking visitors. Many of Venice's most important buildings and historic family palaces can only been seen at their best from the water.

1 Leave the main railway station and turn left, passing the Ferrovia vaporetto stop. Cross over the Ponte degli Scalzi bridge.

Of the 416 bridges in Venice, 300 are made of stone. Only one bridge has no handrails, standard building practice for centuries. Before bridges were even considered, most Venetians moved exclusively by boat or crossed between islands, making use of wooden platforms known as *tolette*.

2 Having crossed the bridge, continue along Calle Lunga Chioverette, then take the first left towards the church of San Simeon Grande. Keep left into Campo San Simeon Grande and walk to the waterside where Riva di Biasio runs along the Grand Canal. The first point of interest is Palazzo Flangini on the opposite side of the canal, to the left of the church of San Geremia e Lucia.

Palazzo Flangini appears a little narrow. It was planned to be twice the size but due to an economic downturn or possibly to a loss of cargo at sea, funds dried up and the initial building project was subsequently downgraded. It is said that exactly one half of the building was demolished out of spite after it was inherited by two arguing brothers of the Flangini family.

3 Keep walking along Riva di Biasio until you arrive at the vaporetto stop of the same name.

WHERE TO EAT

[◎] **TRATTORIA ANTICA TORRE,**
Pescheria Rialto 833;
Tel: 041 523 8315.
This historic inn by the Rialto fish market serves home cooking and is named after the house that was leased to Vielmo Grigis, keeper of the tower. €

[◎] **HARRY'S BAR,**
San Marco 1312, Calle Vallaresso;
Tel: 041 528 5777.
Opened in 1931, Harry's Bar is an obligatory stop. Now one of the world's most celebrated restaurants, the atmosphere of the original bar is still evident. €€

The Riva is named after a butcher who set up shop here. His speciality was a type of sausage with a unique flavour, which he claimed originated from his home in Carnia, Friuli Venezia Giulia. Official records tell us he had been using human flesh in these sausages. This early serial killer came to a gruesome end. He was decapitated, drawn and quartered and his hands chopped off. His house on Riva di Biasio was razed.

4 Board the vaporetto at the Riva di Biaiso stop. Notice Palazzo Gritti on the left, just before Campo San Marcuola. Immediately after the small square on the same side of the bank is Palazzo Vendramin-Calergi, home of the present-day Municipal Venice Casino.

DISTANCE 4 miles (6.4km)

ALLOW 2 hours

START Ferrovia vaporetto stop outside Santa Lucia train station

FINISH Harry's Bar opposite San Marco Vallaresso vaporetto stop

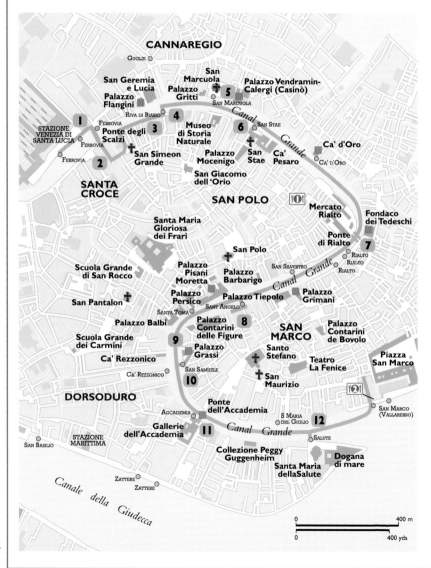

OPPOSITE: PALAZZO FLANGINI WAS ONCE AT THE HEART OF A FAMILY DISPUTE

Disembark at the San Marcuola stop and get a much better look by crossing Campo San Marcuola and turning right over the bridge.

The Casino of Venice was one of many to be established after the fall of the Republic, when gambling was at its height. Look out for a Latin inscription canal side which reads *Non Nobis – Domine Non Nobis* literally 'Not For Our Sake Lord'. It has been attributed to the Vendramin family who wanted to distance themselves from previous ruthless owners whose plottings had led to the murder of Querini Stampalia. Composer Richard Wagner died here in 1883, aged 70.

5 Retrace your steps to pick up the vaporetto again at Campo San Marcuola. The vaporetto will stop at Campo S. Stae. Disembark and consider a short extension crossing the Rio di S. Stae canal to visit Palazzo Ca' Pesaro, which features in Walk 16.

Campo S. Stae was a popular place for another of Venice's traditional trades to display its wares. The prostitutes here were known for their yellow stockings, which may have been flashed at potential customers along the Grand Canal. By the mid-16th century there were 11,000 prostitutes in the city, attracting both sailors and Venice's first tourists.

6 Retrace your steps to pick up the vaporetto once again at San Stae. Following an optional stop at Ca' d'Oro

to visit the gallery of the same name, the vaporetto offers a fine view of the Rialto market before making a sharp right turn that reveals the bulk of the Rialto Bridge. Just before the bridge on the left is Fondaco dei Tedeschi.

The Fondaco dei Tedeschi was headquarters for German, Austrian, Flemish and Hungarian traders who outnumbered all other foreign nationals in the city and were given special privileges by the Republic. The exterior of the building was covered with frescoes by Giorgione (c1477–1510) on the canal side and Titian (c1485–1576) on the other.

7 Having passed under the Rialto Bridge, next stop is San Silvestro. The canal offers a direct view of Palazzo Grimani on the opposite bank.

Today, Palazzo Grimani is home of the Venice Appeal Court. Antonio Grimani had inherited great wealth from his father and his donations to Rome enabled his own son, Domenico, to become a Cardinal. Unfortunately, Doge Antonio was not a great military man and his reign saw the Republic lose much of its Greek colonies to the Turks. He was imprisoned and exiled on the island of Cherso with Domenico carrying his chains, to the derision of the crowd.

8 The vaporetto stop at Sant Angelo offers a chance to disembark on Ramo del Teatro and view a series of fine noble Venetian buildings on the opposite bank. They include Palazzo

Barbarigo, Palazzo Tiepolo, Palazzo Persico and Palazzo Pisani Moretta.

Palazzo Pisani Moretta had the honour of housing what is widely regarded as artist Paolo Veronese's (c1528–1588) finest work, *La Famiglia di Dario ai Piedi di Alessandro*. The painting was sold for cash to the National Portrait Gallery in London in 1870 by Count Vettore Pisani, the last male heir to the noble house. The sum paid was 15,000 gold coins – which he gave to his daughters.

9 Picking up the vaporetto again at Sant Angelo, the Grand Canal takes another sharp bend to the left between Palazzo Balbi and Palazzo Contarini delle Figure before finally straightening out at Palazzo Grassi and the vaporetto stop at San Samuele. The entrance to Palazzo Grassi is just a short walk across Campo San Samuele.

Palazzo Grassi, built for the Grassi family (originally from Chioggia) was recognized as one of the finest of all the noble Venetian palaces. Its façade has become a symbol of the Grand Canal. Today, the palace houses many of the city's best temporary exhibitions.

PALAZZO GRASSI;

www.palazzograssi.it

10 Board the vaporetto at San Samuele and disembark at the Accademia stop before the famous Gallerie dell'Accademia. Cross Campo di Carità to climb onto the Ponte dell'Accademia bridge for one of the classic postcard views of Venice, towards the striking dome of Santa Maria della Salute.

When the Ponte dell'Accademia bridge was constructed in 1854 it was made of iron. The version we see today went up in the 20th century. It was only meant to be a temporary wooden crossing but the permanent stone bridge has never replaced it.

11 Pick up the vaporetto back at the Accademia stop and proceed to the Salute stop.

Every 21 November, one of the city's most lively events, the Festa della Madonna della Salute, is celebrated. A makeshift bridge of boats across the Grand Canal connects the church here to the *sestiere* (quarter) of San Marco.

12 It's a short hop from Salute across Canale di San Marco for the final vaporetto to San Marco Vallaresso. Walk up Calle Vallaresso, perhaps diving into Harry's Bar for a Bellini. This is the area with Venice's finest shops and boutiques.

27

ABOVE: HARRY'S BAR IS THE PLACE TO GO FOR A BELLINI

Where There's Fish There's Gold

The Rialto is a small district with a big history, and still home to Venice's famous vegetable and fish market.

The area around the Rialto market dates from the 11th century when building took off in earnest on and around the island of Luprio. Rialto comes from the words *riva alto* meaning 'high bank', which gives us an idea why the district was popular with the first inhabitants of the lagoon city. The market seems to have begun in nearby Campo San Bartolomeo and moved to Rialto in 1097. By the 13th century, and for the next 300 years, it was perhaps the most cosmopolitan corner of Europe. Following the fall of Byzantium, Venetians mixed with Istrians, Greeks, Albanians, Slavs, French, Hungarians and other nationalities and faiths. In particular, many Jews arrived from Germany, then from Iberia, and aided the commercial growth of Venice through moneylending. This period of cultural exchange also permitted other skills to flourish to the Republic's advantage, including new accounting and book-keeping methods, banking and insurance services.

From the top of the Rialto Bridge, walk down the steps and into Ruga degli Orefici.

At the Ruga degli Orefici (*orefice* means goldsmith) gold, emeralds, rubies, sapphires and other precious stones were worked into finished items, sought after by Ottoman Sultans, European traders and wealthy Venetians alike. It was here that a trader, Niccolò Polo, found himself on a mission. Having returned to Venice in 1295 from a long journey from China with his son, Marco, his wife decided the clothes they had travelled in were not worthy of keeping and donated them to the poor. Unknown to her, fabulous jewels had been sewn inside the lining of a coat to hide them from thieves and robbers on the long journey overland. To get his coat and treasure back Niccolò decided to walk in small circles at the top of the Rialto Bridge, feigning madness. His antics attracted immense curiosity and eventually even the poorest came to look and stare. And along with one of those poor folks came Niccolò's old coat and the treasure he had so effectively hidden away.

2 To the right of Ruga degli Orefici is the small square that is the home of the church of S. Giacomo di Rialto and the statue of Gobbo di Rialto.

The rather lost-looking Gobbo (or hunchback), a granite statue sculpted by Pietro da Salò in 1541, stands opposite the church of San Giacomo di Rialto, a stone's throw from Palazzo Camerlenghi.

WHERE TO EAT

101 MURO VINO E CUCINA,
San Polo 222, Ruga degli Orefici;
Tel: 041 523 7496.
This stylish venue, popular with Venetians, is close to the Rialto Bridge and market. Perfect for a glass of wine with *cicchetti* or a meal that offers traditional Venetian cooking with a modern twist. €€

102 IL DIAVOLO E L'ACQUA SANTA,
Calle della Madonna, 561/B;
Tel: 041 950 102.
A small restaurant with the cozy atmosphere of a pub, but a typically Venetian one. €

103 OSTARIA DAI ZEMEI,
San Polo 1045, near Campo S Aponal;
Tel: 041 520 8596.
A perfect spot – especially for carnivores – for a snack or toasted sandwich complemented by a glass of wine. The simple Parma ham and salami from Emilia go well with a wine list strictly from the northeast corner of Italy. €

The Camerlenghi were the Republic's tax collectors. Non-payers would be invited to spend some time in the cells beneath the building. The Gobbo functioned as a pedestal, from which magistrates would announce public condemnations and other notices. The standard punishment for minor offences

DISTANCE **1 mile (1.6km)**

ALLOW **1 hour 30 minutes**

START **Ponte di Rialto (Rialto Bridge)**

FINISH **Campo S. Aponal in the Rialto district**

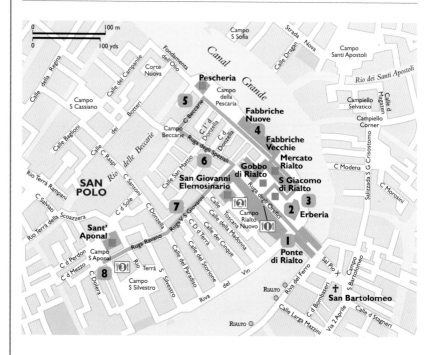

was for the guilty person to run naked from St Mark's Square back to the Rialto through a crowd bearing sticks. This proved to be ideal public humiliation and one after which the penitents would gratefully kiss the Gobbo to thank him that it was all over. So the Gobbo became synonomous with satire and humorous gags against injustice and the nobility. Legend tells us that the church of San Giacomo di Rialto or 'Giocometto' was the first building in the Rialto area constructed as far back as the year 421

and that it could possibly be the oldest church in the city.

3 From the church of S. Giacomo di Rialto, turn right through Sotoportego del Banco Giro by the Erberia dei Tedeschi.

This series of buildings was fundamental to the growth of the Serenissima and the regulation of international trade. At the Banco Giro commercial credit would be thrashed out and insurance

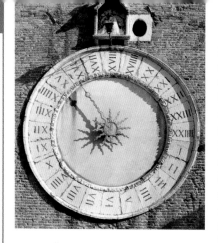

negotiated for voyages. Like any good bet, insurance investments were spread to cover the risk of what could be a highly perilous enterprise. The Serenissima was fundamental in promoting trade and would typically cover all investments made in return for a share of profits. It seems any one voyage had up to 25 backers. Insurance was set at between six and 12 per cent. The sophistication of financing methods increased with the refinement of double account book-keeping by the Venetians and the use of Arabic numerals to replace Roman numbers. In addition, it was helped by the use of the abacus, another importation from the Middle East.

4 Continue the walk by keeping the Banco Giro on your left and proceeding into the magnificently named Campo Cesare Battisti Gia della Bella Vienna. Straight on is the famous Rialto fish market in Campo della Pescaria, reached after passing the Fabbriche Vecchie and Fabbriche Nuove to the right.

Before it gained a reputation for fish the Pescheria was once Venice's public slaughterhouse. It was here that the ill-fated rule of Pietro Candiano IV was ended in the year 976. Following general frustration with his leadership, a rebellion broke out around Palazzo Ducale. A subsequent fire destroyed over 300 houses in the district of San Marco, including the church of San Teodoro, and threatened the Palazzo Ducale. Candiano somehow managed to break out of the building, but was caught amidst the smoke in the atrium of St Mark's Basilica. Pleading for mercy, he was killed on the spot and his body spitefully dumped in the Rialto slaughterhouse. It's all very different today. Look out for the interesting fish and seahorse motifs on the columns of the covered Pescheria. There are also old signs and plaques indicating buying and selling regulations over the centuries; for example, sardines were required to be at least 3in (7cm) long.

RIALTO FISH MARKET;
www.venicevenetogourmet.com

5 Leave the fish market by Calle Beccarie. This will take you into Campo Beccarie.

The Beccarie is now home to Venice's traditional meat market in the area where a slaughterhouse and market has existed since the 9th century. The market was rebuilt with stones from the house of Querini, who was decapitated following a failed coup in 1310. Near Campo Beccarie, the Venetian couriers or pony express had its headquarters at the spot where today's popular 'Alle Poste Vece' restaurant stands.

6 Walk along Ruga degli Speziali. At the small crossroads where Ruga degli Speziali meets Ruga degli Orefici, turn right to find the church of San Giovanni Elemosinario on the left.

The entrance to the church of San Giovanni Elemosinario is now somewhat hidden by the stalls and general activity of the Rialto market, but it was once an important reference point for local traders and artisan associations who provided funds and their time to buy precious artistic works, which can still be seen inside.

ASSOCIAZIONE CHIESE DI VENEZIA;

www.chorusvenezia.org

7 Continue along Ruga V. S. Giovanni and into Ruga Ravano which runs into Rio Terra S. Aponal.

The church of Sant'Aponal was one of many suppressed by the French during Napoleon's occupation. It became a political prison and is now closed. In nearby Calle della Madonna, one of Venice's most significant historical episodes is remembered. In 1177, Pope Alexander III had become a political refugee, having fled Rome and Holy Roman Emperor, Frederick Barbarossa. He eventually made it to Venice but remained incognito in the city for six months, sleeping rough a stone's throw from the church of Sant'Aponal. His identity remained a mystery until

he was recognized by a Frenchman, who informed the Serenissima. News raced back to Rome and an infuriated Barbarossa dispatched a fleet of 65 galleys, led by his son Otto and supported by his Genovese allies, to bring his rightful prisoner back. In a memorable Venetian victory, Otto was captured. The Republic took the moral and diplomatic high ground and engineered peace between the Pope and Barbarossa for the return of his son. In gratitude, the Pope gave the Doge a wedding ring to acknowledge Venice's domination of the Adriatic Sea. A small statue of the sleeping Pope in the *sotoportego* (small arched alley) commemorates this event.

8 The walk finishes amidst the hustle and bustle of the Rialto district. The well of Campo S. Aponal is a useful surface on which to spread the map to get one's bearings. Walk 16, 'Stories between Three Museums', begins here.

LIFE CONTINUES QUIETLY IN THE CANNAREGIO DISTRICT

The Ghetto Opens its Doors

This very easy walk offers an introduction to the Cannaregio district of Venice, little frequented by most tourists.

Many believe the original Jewish presence in Venice was initially limited to the Isola Spinalunga (to the south of the city), so that the islands became known as Giudecca (*Guidei* is Italian for Jews), but there is no hard evidence for this. What is certain is that Jews were granted a licence to lend money in 1366 and at that time permitted freedom of movement in the city. The community prospered along with the Republic, their liquidity particularly appreciated in times of war. The birth of the Ghetto in 1516 was prompted by the large influx of Jews into Venice, fleeing from the mainland following the institution of the League of Cambrai by Pope Julius II in 1509. Granted a small island in the Cannaregio district, the Jewish zone became known as the Ghetto Nuovo, the word 'geto' imported by new arrivals from Germany, eventually becoming hardened into 'gheto'. The area was protected by the Serenissima from religious zealots, but there was always an undercurrent of racism.

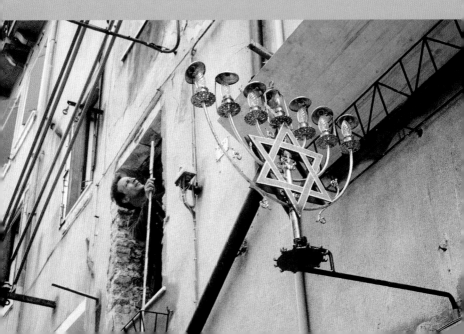

From the Ponte Brazzo, continue along Fondamenta dei Mori as it runs along the Rio della Sensa canal. As Fondamenta dei Mori leads into Fondamenta della Sensa, it enters the Parish of Sant'Alvise. Here, stop at Calle delle Muneghe on the right.

'Muneghe' is a reference to nuns, and looking along the *calle* across the Rio di S. Alvise, the convent and church of Sant'Alvise can be clearly seen in the near distance. Founded in 1388 by Augustinian nuns as a small hermitage, the church gained a much higher profile when it acquired the relics of the Flagellation in 1456. In 1735 the nuns eventually commissioned Tiepolo (1696–1770) to paint his masterpiece on this theme and the work of art still hangs in the church. The costumes worn by the characters in the painting show how the artist had been influenced by the many melodramatic theatre performances that were common in Venice at the time.

Continue along Fondamenta di Sensa and turn right at Calle dei Riformati. From here, cross over the Ponte Bonaventura and turn right again into Fondamenta dei Riformati until you reach Campo di S. Alvise.

The church of Sant'Alvise is named after the patron saint of Toulouse in France, Alvise being the Venetian equivalent of Louis. He appeared in a dream to patrician lady Antonia Venier in 1383, showing her where a new convent should be built. Venier funded the building

herself and when it was complete she lived in the annex. The very plain exterior in bare brick is unique in Venice, with the 15th-century statue of St Louis one of the few details.

ASSOCIAZIONE CHIESE DI VENEZIA;
www.chorusvenezia.org

Leave Campo di S. Alvise by crossing the bridge into Calle del Capitello and continuing over a second bridge leading into Calle de la Malvasia. Ignore a third bridge and turn right into Fondamenta degli Ormesini.

The Fondamenta takes its name from *ormesin*, the printed silk originating from the Hormuz zone of the Gulf of Persia. Workshops producing curtains, cushions and quilts from this material were located here. After passing the Antica Mola Trattoria, keep an eye out for a plaque marking the spot where master gondolier Renato Bona worked carving *forcole* (rowlocks) and oars for gondolas. The trattoria celebrates his life with pictures and trophies.

DISTANCE 1.5 miles (2.4km)

ALLOW 2 hours 15 minutes

START Ponte Brazzo near Casa Tintoretto

FINISH Ponte Tre Archi over the Cannaregio Canal

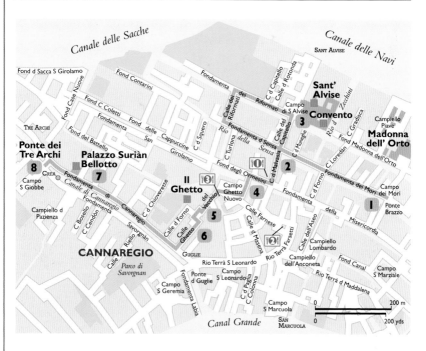

4 Leave Fondamenta degli Ormesini by crossing the first bridge on the left into Campo Ghetto Nuovo.

The first nucleus of Jews to be moved to the New Ghetto consisted of Germans, arrivals from southern France, and those from central and southern Italy. They were joined at a later date by two new groups, the 'Ponentini' from Spain and Portugal and the 'Levantini' from the Ottoman Empire, some of whom were also confined to the Old Ghetto.

The latter enjoyed more favourable treatment by the Republic thanks to their importance in international trade. Nevertheless, various constrictions and rules were strictly enforced. For example, the community would retreat behind closed doors during Christmas and other Christian celebrations. Outside of the Ghetto Nuovo, Jews had to be visible and identifiable by a yellow 'O' sewn onto their clothes, although this was later modified to wearing a yellow cap. Finally, the Jews' trade with the wider

city could only extend to moneylending and medicine; on no account were they allowed to possess real estate. In Campo Ghetto Nuovo you can still see a sign, *Banco Rosso*, indicating one of the moneylender's positions. The continuing prosperity of the community attracted many more Jews to Venice and the community spilled over into the Ghetto Vecchio and Ghetto Nuovissimo.

5 Exit the Campo del Ghetto by crossing over the bridge into Calle Barucchi, which then leads into the Old Ghetto or Ghetto Vecchio along Calle del Ghetto Vecchio.

The most famous person to live in the Old Ghetto was Leon da Modena or Judah Aryeh (1571–1648). A major intellectual figure of the early modern Italian Jewish community, he was a complex, intriguing personality, famous among contemporary European Christians as well as Jews. Modena produced an autobiography which

documents in poignant detail the turbulent life of his family. His text is well known to Jewish scholars and offers a wealth of historical material about daily Jewish family life, religion, crime and punishment, as well as the influence of kabbalistic mysticism. Modena describes his fascination with astrology and alchemy – important parts of Jewish and general culture of the 17th century. He also portrays his struggle against poverty and compulsive gambling, which, cleverly punning on a biblical verse, he called the 'sin of Judah'. In addition, the book contains accounts of Modena's sorrow over his three sons: the death of the eldest from the poisonous fumes of his own alchemical laboratory, the brutal murder of the youngest, and the exile of the remaining son.

6 Pass through the small Campiello de le Scuole and continue along Calle del Ghetto Vecchio. The Jewish zone ends at Sotoportego de Ghetto, which opens onto Fondamenta di Cannaregio.

ABOVE: FOOTBRIDGES LINK THE GHETTO NUOVO AND THE GHETTO VECCHIO

There are five synagogues located in the area of the Ghetto: the Great German Synagogue or Scuola Grande Tedesca; the Scuola Canton, most probably founded by Southern French Jews; Scuola Italiana and, in the New Ghetto Square, the Scuola Grande Spagnola and Scuola Levantina.
Two of them still regularly open for the 450 or more Jews still residing in Venice. In the Old Ghetto (Campiello delle Scuole) take note of the two extremely tall buildings, still inhabited today. With very little land available there was only one direction in which to build – up. Steep staircases lead up seven floors, without lifts.

7 After Palazzo Surian Bellotto, continue until you reach the large Ponte dei Tre Archi or the Bridge of Three Arches, the only three-arched bridge in Venice, built by Andrea 'Tyrant' Tirali in 1688.

Palazzo Surian Bellotto was the seat of the French Embassy. Cardinal De Bernis lived here and, with his friend Giacomo Casanova (1725–98) plotted many infamous escapades. The Ambassador's secretary was Jean Jacques Rousseau (1712–78), who had a reputation for sexual deviancy that even Venetian courtesans wanted to stay clear of. One in particular was a certain prostitute known as Zulieta, who let her feelings be known while 'entertaining' Rousseau in her bedroom. Pointing two loaded pistols at Rousseau she said, 'I can endure their caresses, but I don't intend to endure

WHERE TO EAT

🍴 TRATTORIA ANTICA MOLA,
Cannaregio 2800, Fondamenta d'Ormesini;
No phone.
A great place for a down-to-earth lunch of classic Venetian pasta. The trattoria has close associations with the gondoliers and gondola tradition. Dessert is strictly homemade. €

🍴 BENTIGODI OSTERIA DA ANDREA,
Cannaregio 1423, Rio Terrá Farsetti;
Tel: 041 716 269.
Official Venice walking tour guides rate this as the best pizzeria in Venice. It is located between the New Ghetto and San Marcuola. €

🍴 RISTORANTE AI QUATTRO RUSTEGHI,
Cannaregio 2888, Campo del Ghetto Nuovo;
Tel: 041 715 160.
An informal and calm atmosphere in which to enjoy typical Venetian dishes with origins in the Levant. €€

their insults. Little John, leave the ladies alone, and study mathematics'.

8 Finish the walk by crossing Ponte Tre Archi. Either take the vaporetto at the Crea stop or start Walk 18, 'Terra Firma and Terra Veneta', both of which finish at Santa Lucia railway station.

Murano –
Islands of Glass

The trip to the heart of Murano is best scheduled for the morning to conclude with a leisurely lunch before returning to Venice.

Murano is made up of five small islands just half a mile (1km) from Venice. It can be reached from the Fondamenta Nouve and the various vaporetti can drop the day visitor back at diverse points across the city, even as far as St Mark's Square. Murano really is the island of glass. The industry transferred here in the 13th century when the demand for precious hand-blown glass objects grew to a phenomenal extent. The Republic decided it was wise to concentrate the numerous workshops, and more importantly the furnaces, in a unique space away from the main centre of the city. The trade and skills of the artisans reached their peak in the 16th century. At this time, these artists were held in the same high esteem as a lawyer, doctor or notary, and thought of as suitable marriage material for daughters of noble families. Murano was always a preferred retreat for patricians who built spacious palaces or villas with beautiful gardens. Unfortunately, since the Napoleonic invasion of 1795 little remains of these palaces.

Having arrived in Murano by boat and alighted at the Faro (lighthouse) vaporetto stop, begin your visit by walking along Viale Garibaldi.

There is no gradual introduction to the glass-making tradition of Murano for those arriving on the island. As soon as you navigate the short gangplank and step onto the island, the factories, furnaces and other telltale indications of glass manufacture are close by. Perhaps the most fabulous reception ever given to a visitor to Murano was that bestowed on King Henry III of France in the 16th century. He was escorted by 60 senators in gondolas and greeted on the island by a guard of honour of 60 halberdiers dressed in sky blue and orange silk uniforms. Forty young Venetian nobles then met him outside the Palace of Bartolomeo Cappello, which was adorned with gold tapestries for the occasion. Inside, Doge Mocenigo himself welcomed the king then travelled with him to San Nicolò di Lido in his galley, powered by 400 oarsmen fitted out in blue and yellow taffeta.

2 Where Viale Garibaldi meets the canal turn left along Fondamenta D. Manin. At the Ponte S. Chiara, double back over the other side of the canal along Fondamenta dei Vetrai to the church of S. Pietro Martire.

Both the church of San Pietro Martire (St Peter the Martyr) and the Scuola Grande di San Giovanni Evangelista in Venice were constructed in 1348, the same year that a serious earthquake shook the wooden

WHERE TO EAT

RESTAURANT B,
Campiello Pescheria 4;
Tel: 041 527 4957.
Restaurant B combines good food in a stylish atmosphere and is situated in its own square, away from crowds and in the heart of the Murano shopping district. €€

RISTORANTE AI PIANTA LEONI,
Riva Longo 25;
Tel: 041 736 794.
Traditional Murano cooking with a choice of fish and meat dishes, served in a semi-informal environment on the edge of the canal. €€

TRATTORIA VALMARANA,
Fondamenta Navagero Andrea 31;
Tel: 041 739 313.
This small trattoria specializes in fish dishes from soups to fry-ups. It is located in a quiet corner of Murano, set apart from other buildings, and not far from the Glass Museum. €€

foundations of Venice in January and the Black Death broke out in the islands just weeks later, eventually killing three-fifths of the population. Disappointingly, the 10 large chandeliers of the church are all in plain glass.

3 Exiting the church, turn left into Fondamenta da Mula, noting the small tower in Campo S. Stefano on the

43

DISTANCE 2 miles (3.2km)

ALLOW 3 hours

START Faro vaporetto stop in Murano

FINISH Navagero vaporetto stop in Murano

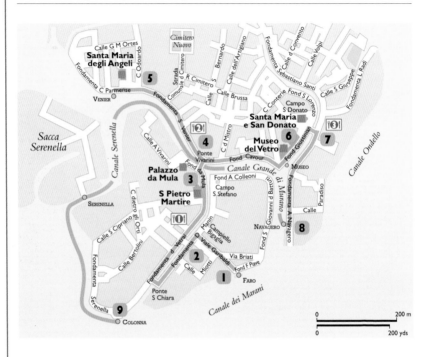

other side of the canal. Keep on Fondamenta da Mula as it bears left until you reach the Ponte Vivarini bridge, which crosses the Grand Canal of Murano.

The Palazzo da Mula is one of the few summer noble palaces to survive to the 21st century more or less intact. It dates from the 12th century and was immortalized in paint by Claude Monet in 1908. The original painting hangs in the National Gallery of Art in Washington, D.C. All along the Fondamanta you can't

move for Murano glass shops alternating with larger showrooms.

4 Having crossed the Ponte Vivarini, turn left onto Fondamenta Sebastiano Venier and continue the full length of the Fondamenta to the church of Santa Maria degli Angeli.

The church of Santa Maria degli Angeli was the location for one of Venice's most legendary stories, featuring the city's most infamous character, Casanova.

OPPOSITE: THE CHURCH OF SAN PIETRO MARTIRE IN MURANO

A tale of love and seduction, it was here that Casanova consummated his affair with the mysterious '*monaca di clausura*' or nun. A small wooden bridge leads to the entrance of the convent, where the nun would leave in the company of a female companion. Both would be whisked off by gondola with the philanderer hiding his identity behind a mask.

5 Backtrack along Fondamenta Venier to the Ponte Vivarini once again. Do not cross back over the bridge but continue along Fondamenta Cavour until it turns sharp left into Fondamenta Giustinian. The Museo del Vetro (Glass Museum) entrance is on the left.

The Glass Museum is inside Palazzo Giustinian. It contains fabulous examples of glass objects dating from the 1st century BC. Priceless Venetian works from the 15th to 19th centuries include a fine wedding cup from 1480. One very special object is a wine glass found intact following the collapse of the bell tower (Campanile) in St Mark's Square in 1902. Along with a large bell and a statue of the Archangel Gabriel, the three items have become symbols of the immortality of the lagoon city, if not the defunct Republic. Every year on 14 July the glass is taken out for a toast as it was when used to celebrate the building of the first bell tower in the 16th century.

CONSORZIO PROMOVETRO MURANO;
www.muranoglass.com

6 Leaving the Glass Museum, turn left and follow Fondamenta Giustinian as the Fondamenta opens into Campiello

Cavalieri di V. Veneto, which in turn becomes Campo S. Donato.

The 12th-century Cathedral of San Donato was previously the Church of Santa Maria built in the year 999. What we see today is as old as the Basilica of St Mark in Venice and can be compared with the Romanesque Churches of Ravenna. It is also one of the largest in the lagoon. The interior has stunning Venetian Byzantine floors of marble and glass mosaics, manufactured in the oldest kilns on the island. The interior also boasts artistic works by Bellini and Veronese.

7 Leave Campo S. Donato opposite the church. Cross the bridge over the canal and turn right along Fondamenta Navagero to the Navagero vaporetto stop.

When leaving Murano, think of Tommaso Zustinian who did the very same in 1510. This was the period of the League of Cambrai, whose intention was to destroy the political, commercial and military might of Venice. Disturbed by events, Zustinian's next stop was the hermitage of Camaldoli near Florence. After a year of contemplation he was joined by Pietro Querini, a member of the so-called cenacolo (Last Supper) of Murano. Bravely, the two decided to present a document arguing for the reform of the Church to newly elected Pope Leon X who was both a Tuscan and a Medici. The document, called the Libellus ad Leonem X, proposed the questioning of clerics who

appeared ignorant of liturgical rites and ceremony, as well as the elimination of sermons which were all spectacle and no substance. Nothing came of the document, but a third member of the cenacolo, Gasparo Contarini, kept in touch with his fellow thinkers. When Pope Paul III succeeded Leon X, he was made a cardinal and subsequently pushed through his Consilium de Emendanda Ecceslia.

8 The vaporetto takes a wonderful long route back through the Murano Grand Canal and under the Ponte Vivarini, then turning left into Canale Serenella before heading into the lagoon after the Colonna mooring.

It seems Napoleon liked gardens more than he did churches. During French rule, between 1806 and 1810, Venice lost numerous monasteries and churches through suppression and wagons full of art were taken away to Paris or auctioned elsewhere. Incredibly, a total of 72 religious buildings were ordered to be completely demolished. Fortunately, one of those that survived was the church of San Michele standing on its own island between Murano and Venice. It was here, beside the church, that a cemetery was built and where people of note such as poet Ezra Pound (1885–1972) and composer Igor Stravinsky (1882–1971) were laid to rest.

9 Finish by taking the vaporetto back to Fondamenta Nuove. Alternatively, some public transport vessels proceed to the Grand Canal via the Cannaregio Canal. Disembark at your port of choice.

SANTA MARIA E DONATO, MURANO

Burano – Island of Lace

A visit to the island of Burano is especially good in the warmer months when you can combine shopping for lace with an alfresco fish supper.

The first inhabitants of Burano were exiles from the Roman town of Altino on the mainland. They fled the invading Longobards (Lombards) from Northern Europe twice, first in 453 and then definitively in 635, when Altino was razed to the ground by King Rotari and his men. They brought the memory of their old home with them and it is thought that Burano or Boreamum was named after one of the six access gates or zones of the Roman municipium – although other theories abound. Maybe Burano is simply named after *burie*, a medieval term for waterway or perhaps it may not even be the original Burano. In the 10th century, the constant battle with the elements and the lagoon led to the erosion of the original settlement, forcing the inhabitants to seek yet another new home in Burano Nuovo. What is clear is that today's Burano was a series of five islets, which over time became consolidated, culminating with the filling in of the canal that now forms the main square of the town.

To get to the island of Burano, take the vaporetto from Fondamenta Nuove in the Castello district of Venice. The vessel takes around 40 minutes to navigate the lagoon. Arriving in Burano, disembark and turn right. Walk towards the brightly coloured houses along Strada di Corte Comare.

The houses range in colour from green and sky blue tones to reds, oranges and garish pink. To understand the practical reason for their colourful display it is best to see the houses in winter, when the mist reduces visibility in the lagoon to a minimum. Painting the house fronts in bright colours meant that the buildings were more visible to returning fisherman in the days before artificial light provided illumination. As a deep blue tile in the wall of one of the houses along Fondamenta Cavanelle states, in white verse, 'Color is like Music. It uses shorter way (sic) to come to our Senses to wake our emotions.'

2 Reaching the end of Strada di Corte Comare, turn left. Continue through Corte Comare.

Corte Comare is where the fishermen's houses open up into a wide court or square. Even today, Burano retains the atmosphere of a down-to-earth, hardworking fishing village. On the right, just before the bridge and high up on one of the exterior walls of a house, is a statue of the Virgin Mary and the infant Jesus offering protection to those who brave the sea. The blue and white colours of the figures contrast spectacularly with the bright pink walls of the building.

3 Cross over the bridge, which links Fondamenta Cavanella to Fondamenta Cao Moleca. Turn immediately right and continue until you reach the old fish market by the lagoon.

From this vantage point the lagoon stretches towards the islands of Mazzorbo, Murano and eventually Venice, and looks every bit like a peaceful spot for a fine day's fishing. However, it was not so on the 24 September 1867, when a huge storm blew up, creating exceptionally high tides and destroying 240 houses and killing eight Buranese people. A plaque on the wall of St Martin's Church above a statue to Pope John Paul II commemorates this devastating event.

51

DISTANCE **2 miles (3.2km)**

ALLOW **3 hours 30 minutes**

START **Burano vaporetto stop in Burano**

FINISH **Burano vaporetto stop in Burano**

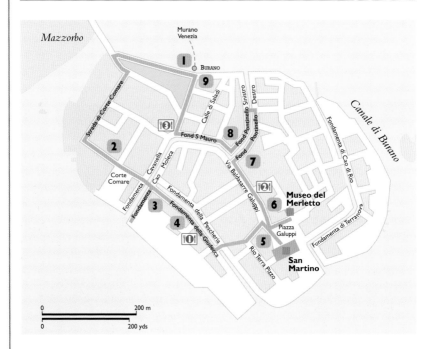

4 Backtrack along Fondamenta Cao Moleca and turn first right into Fondamenta della Giudecca. At Corte Novello, cross over the new bridge and continue straight on, until you see a curious opening through two connecting houses. This is Calle della Providenza and it cuts through into Rio Terra Pizzo, which exits in the heart of Burano.

The heart of Burano is dedicated to lace shops. Look closely above them and you will notice the fading signs of old lace schools where the girls of the island were trained. The working of lace on the island of Burano is inextricably linked to the centuries-old skill of making and repairing fishing nets, although some insist that the techniques needed to produce fine lace were imported to the lagoon from Byzantium. In any case, lace items became immensely fashionable from the 15th century, not least due to the enthusiasm of Giovanna Dandolo, the wife of Doge Pasquale Malipiero. Even King Richard III of England demanded

that his robes be adorned with Burano lace for his coronation in 1483.

5 After a wander around the shops, head for Chiesa San Martino. Cross Piazza Galuppi to the Museo del Merletto or Lace Museum.

Beneath the altar of the church of St Martin is a marble sarcophagus containing the remains of the island's patron saints. It is worth a visit before crossing over the square to the Lace Museum. The small oratory on the left, just after the exit of the church, is dedicated to Santa Barbara of Nicomedia in Turkey. The saint's relics were brought here from Constantinople by Maria di Bisanzio at the turn of the first millennium. They went initially to the island of Torcello, then came to Burano in 1811. Their arrival here established a trend for many more such relics to be brought to Venice from the Holy Land, and these still adorn many Venetian churches today.

6 Exit the Merletto Museum by turning right and right again into Via Baldassarre Galuppi.

Palazzo Galuppi is named after Baldassarre Galuppi (1706–85), who in the second half of the 18th century taught music in the Ospedale della Pieta in Venice, a church linked to composer Antonio Vivaldi (1678–1741). Galuppi was also a contemporary of Carlo Goldoni (1707–93) and Giacomo Casanova (1725–98). His statue takes pride of place in the main square. The young Galuppi was considered a prodigy, standing out from the rest of his contemporaries in this most hardworking of islands. A famous quotation by Galuppi confirms his attitude to life: 'He who has no nose has little need of a handkerchief'.

7 At the end of Via Baldassarre Galuppi there is a wooden bridge. Turn right once you reach this point and proceed along Fondamenta Pontinello Destro until a second bridge crosses back over the canal onto Fondamenta Pontinello Sinistro. Backtrack along the other side of the canal until you reach Fondamenta San Mauro.

ABOVE: THE MUSEO DEL MERLETTO HAS DISPLAYS OF PRECIOUS LACE ITEMS

This is one of the most scenic points of Burano and it contrasts well with the open spaces of the first half of the walk. The houses are just as colourful as the canal eventually twists back to the fish market. Interestingly, the street names and squares in Burano are not written in Venetian dialect as in Venice, but in Italian.

8 Turn right to continue along Fondamenta San Mauro until reaching a stone bridge. Here, turn right into Calle S. Mauro through Via di Mazzorbo to the vaporetto stop.

The vaporetto ride back to Venice passes the island of Mazzorbo and other small plots of land visible or not depending on the level of the lagoon. On the return journey, keep this short myth in mind: A long time ago, a maiden called Dolfina lived on the island of Burano. She was fair with a pale complexion and a young fisherman called Polo soon fell in love with her. The couple decided to get married, but fishing was considered a lowly occupation, only guaranteeing a meagre income. Polo did not even have enough money for an engagement present. One day, while out fishing, he noticed something had become trapped in his nets. It was seaweed encrusted with marine salt, curiously beautiful and the perfect gift for his beloved. Impressed, Dolfina wondered how she could preserve this brittle treasure. She took a needle and thread and copied the seaweed's design. Weaving and stitching and securing each end of the thread with tiny knots, she created a light and sturdy

WHERE TO EAT

🍴 **TRATTORIA AL GATTO NERO,**
Fondamenta Giudecca 88;
Tel: 041 730 120.
Widely acknowledged as the best restaurant in Burano and one of the best in Venice, the Black Cat was established in 1946 and specializes in fresh fish. €€€

🍴 **TRATTORIA DA PRIMO,**
Piazza Galuppi 285;
Tel: 041 735 550.
Run by a fishing family, this traditional trattoria serves such dishes as *risotto alla Buranella*, mixed grills and typical Burano sweets and desserts at modest prices. €€

🍴 **RIVA ROSA,**
Via San Mauro 296;
Tel: 041 730 850.
A plush dining spot, which is both an elegant restaurant and wine bar, with a splendid picturesque view of the main canal cutting its way through Burano. €€

net. It was a masterpiece of perfection, and the exquisite and intricate Burano lace was born.

9 From Burano there is a dedicated vaporetto that goes to Torcello, the first of the Venetian islands to be inhabited permanently and which boasts the oldest building in the lagoon, the cathedral of Santa Maria dell'Assunta.

The Island of Reform

In summer, a walk in the Giudecca offers scant shade. But it is a great place for an aperitif, gazing at St Mark's Square as the sun sets.

Originally known as Spinalunga or 'long spine', Giudecca is a series of eight small islands stretching about 1 mile (1.6km) and separated from the rest of Venice, and the *sestiere* (district) of Dorsoduro in particular, by the Giudecca Canal. Until recently it was never much of a desired address or real estate investment. Historically the island was home to exiled nobles, Venice's problem children and small-time criminals, as well as small factories and boatyards. Giudecca's recent renewal is symbolized by the Mulino Stucky, a converted flour mill and icon of industrial archaeology that has recently been converted into a hotel and congress centre after years of abandon. The area is now sought after, and Elton John has allegedly bought a little place along the Fondamenta delle Zitelle. Public funding is financing new showrooms for glass, paper, metal and other artisan crafts, and the world's first gondola museum is also planned.

| Take the vaporetto from the Zattere stop on the Fondamenta Zattere ai Gesuiti in Dorsoduro and disembark at Palanca Giudecca. Turn right along Fondamenta S. Eufemia to the church of Sant'Eufemia.

The church of S.Eufemia dates from the 9th century and has been modified on numerous occasions. Columns dating from the 11th century are still visible, but it is a modest building compared to the Basilica of Sant'Eufemia in Grado and the mother of all the Venetian churches.

2 Turn left into Fondamenta Rio di S. Eufemia along the canal to Campo S. Cosmo. Where the Fondamenta meets the bridge, stop and look over to Rio delle Convertite on the other side.

The scenic view from the bridge into Rio delle Convertite has been the location for many films. This district of disused factories and shipyards, including the original Dreher beer factory, is a peaceful and quiet spot. The name of the Rio delle Convertite refers to an oratory that housed prostitutes and disgraced women who wished to become nuns and leave their past life behind. The first rector of the former Convento delle Convertite was a priest from Valcamonica in the Lombardy Alps. He was executed between the two columns in St Mark's Square for having abused many of the women in his charge and trust. The building is now a short-term women's prison where the predominantly foreign inmates produce theatre props

WHERE TO EAT

[O] I FIGLI DELLE STELLE,
Giudecca 70/71, near Zitelle
vaporetto stop;
Tel: 041 523 0004.
Modern and elegant restaurant with a superb view of Venice from the Zitelle. On the menu are new interpretations of traditional Mediterranean flavours. €€

[O] RISTORANTE MISTRA,
Giudecca 212a, off Fondamenta
S. Giacomo;
Tel: 041 522 0743.
To get to the Mistra requires an unusual walk through a boatyard. The restaurant is located on the upper floor of a warehouse, and the view of the southern lagoon is superb. The menu is based on fresh ingredients of the day. €€

and handbags, as well as cultivating a small plot of land. In fact, one of the Giudecca's oldest incarnations was as a market garden.

3 From Campo S. Cosma walk away from the bridge and turn left, passing the Ex Chiesa dei S.S. Cosma e Damiano and into Campazzo S. Cosma, which leads back to Fondamenta S. Eufemia and the Giudecca Canal. Continue straight along Fondamenta del Ponte Piccolo to Rio del Ponte Lungo, over the Ponte Lungo that crosses it, and into Fondamenta San Giacomo.

DISTANCE **2.5 miles (4km)**

ALLOW **2 hours**

START **Zattere vaporetto stop by the Giudecca Canal**

FINISH **San Giorgio vaporetto stop on Isola San Giorgio Maggiore**

Beside the Ex Chiesa dei S.S. Cosma e Damiano is another reform institute, inside a converted woollen factory. Ponte Lungo is located at the mid point of the walk and crosses the wide Rio del Ponte Lungo that offers a convenient shortcut for larger vessels to pass from one side of Giudecca to the other. It also allowed nobles to reach their gaming lodges and homes, which typically face the south bank, a tranquil garden area with spectacular sunsets, in contrast to the strictly working class nature of most of the area. Along the canal is the old Junghans factory and bunker that at one time produced watches, then bombs.

Today it has been converted into the small Junghans Theatre, which seats only 150 people in an intimate atmosphere.
JUNGHANS THEATRE;
www.teatrojunghans.it

4 Follow Fondamenta S. Giacomo in the Quartiere San Giacomo until you reach Campo del Redentore and the Redentore Church.

The nearby monastery of Santa Croce suffered during the plague of 1464 but was central to the construction of the famous Redentore Church. Legend has it that four nuns had died of the plague and another was seriously ill, when a knight appeared at the monastery asking for a glass of water. Thanking the sister who gave it to him and telling her to have faith in God, the knight assured her that the plague would soon pass and the sick nun and everyone else would survive. At that point the sister recognized the knight as St Sebastian. He promptly disappeared. However, his words were prophetic and the well at the monastery became known as the Pozzo di San Sebastian. The waters helped many during the plague of 1576 and inspired the building of the Redentore. Designed by Andrea Palladio (1508–80), the project was completed under the supervision of Antonio Da Ponte, the architect of the

ABOVE: ONE OF THE EVANGELIST STATUES ON SAN GIORGIO MAGGIORE

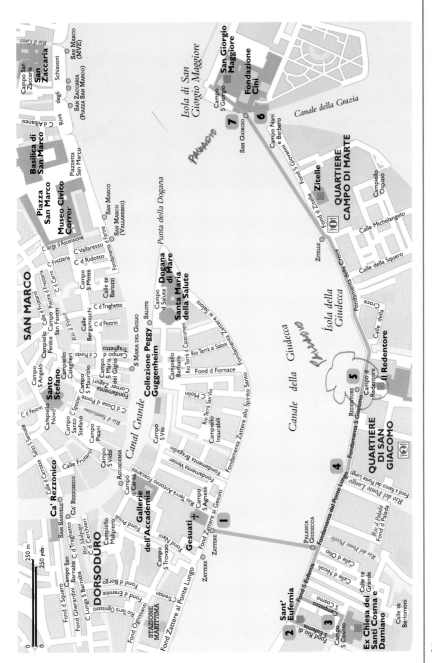

250 m
250 yds

DORSODURO

Ca' Rezzonico
Ca' Rezzonico

SAN SAMUELE

SAN MARCO

Santo
Stefano

Gallerie
dell'Accademia

Collezione Peggy
Guggenheim

Piazza
San Marco

Museo Civico
Correr

Basilica di
San Marco

San
Zaccaria

SAN ZACCARIA (MVE)

SAN ZACCARIA
(PIAZZA SAN MARCO)

Schiavoni

Riva degli

C d'Albanesi

Piazzetta
San Marco

SAN MARCO
(VALLARESSO)

Clarga d'Ascensione

C Frezzaria

C d'Corso

C Vallaresso

C d Ridotto

Campo
S Moisè

Calle te
Barozzi

Fondamenta d'Farine

Punta della Dogana

Dogana
di Mare

Campo
d Salute

Santa Maria
della Salute

SALUTE

S MARIA DEL GIGLIO

Campo
d Canto

Fondamenta Venier

Fondamenta Bragadin

Campo
S Vio

Campo
S Agnese

Gesuati

ZATTERE

Fondamenta Zattere al Ponte Lungo

STAZIONE
MARITTIMA

**Sant'
Eufemia**

Fond Rio di
S Eufemia

Campo
S Cosmo

**Ex Chiesa del
Santi Cosma e
Damiano**

Calle te
Berlomoni

**QUARTIERE
DI SAN
GIACOMO**

Il Redentore

Isola della Giudecca

Canale della Giudecca

Isola di San
Giorgio Maggiore

**San Giorgio
Maggiore**

**Fondazione
Cini**

SAN GIORGIO

Campo
S Giorgio

Canale della Grazia

Zitelle

ZITELLE

**QUARTIERE
CAMPO DI MARTE**

Calle Michelangelo

Calle della Squero

1
2
3
4
5
6
7

present Rialto Bridge. The church was consecrated in 1592. It is from here every third Saturday in July that the Redentore Festival is celebrated, when a huge number of boats or *chiatta* form a temporary bridge across the Giudecca Canal to the Zattere. Outside the steps of the church 30 men departed for Croatia using the famous underwater M.A.S. motorbikes to blow up Austrian defences in the last year of World War I. A small monument lists the heroes. **ASSOCIAZIONE CHIESE DI VENEZIA;** www.chorusvenezia.org

5 Exit the church and turn right onto Fondamenta della Croce. Continue to the Zitelle vaporetto stop that links Giudecca to San Giorgio Maggiore Island.

The vaporetto stop is named after the Convent and Church of San Maria della Presentazione, commonly known as the church of the Zitelle. It dates from 1599 and was an institute for young girls from poor families. The great flood and storm of 15 February 1340 inspired a legend: as lightning struck a man asked the fisherman for a passage to the island from Ponte della Paglia near Palazzo Ducale. There a second man, a knight, requested that the boat head to the Abbey of San Niccolò Lido where a third person, a Papal bishop, jumped on board. The three then ordered the boat to head against the ferocious wind into the high swell of the lagoon to confront a huge black ship with ripped sails. The ship was captained by the devil himself, to whom the three men held up a crucifix and three times made the sign of the cross. The black ship

sank and the storm miraculously abated. The three men were saints Nicholas, George and Mark the Evangelist. A 16th-century painting of the legend can be seen in the Gallerie dell'Accademia.

6 Disembarking at San Giorgio, stop at the gates of the Cini Foundation.

Once known as the island of cypress trees, the island of San Giorgio was a Benedictine stronghold but had been known from Roman times as Insula Memnia after a noble Roman family who owned land here. It was from this spot that Gerardo Sagredo departed for Hungary to become Bishop of Csnad. Killed in September 1046 protecting the son of King Stefano of Hungary, he became a martyr and the patron saint of Hungary. The church of San Giorgio we see today is by Palladio, who also designed the '*Chiostro* (cloisters) of Cypress trees' on the island in 1618. It was here the Papal conclave voted in 1800 to elect Cardinal Barnaba Chiaramonti as Pope Pius VII; Rome was occupied by French troops at the time. The French also suppressed the convent at the beginning of the 19th century and in 1951, the island was given in concession to the Cini Foundation. You can see St Mark's Square from the piazza in front of the church. **FONDAZIONE GIORGIO CINI;** www.cini.it

7 Return to the Zattere stop in the district of Dorsoduro by vaporetto to begin either Walk 23, 'Rising Tides and Watermarks' or Walk 11, 'The Last Gondola Maker'.

LEGENDS SURROUND THE ISLAND OF SAN GIORGIO MAGGIORE

The Plague needs no Passport

This is certainly not a walk you would have wanted to take in 1630, when the pernicious great plague broke out across the city.

Napoleon was perhaps Venice's only real invader, apart from the plague, but both had devastating effects. In a city with no sewers and whose economy and growth relied on overseas trade and the need to import basic foodstuffs, plagues and other epidemics were inevitable. The Black Death, or bubonic plague, of the mid-14th century hit Venice hard, as it did much of Europe. Three-fifths of the population of the Republic died, a population drop Venice could barely survive. Anticipating future disasters, the city set up its three *savi*, or magistrates, to look after the Serenissima's sanitary situation. Their job was to try and prevent disease, or at worst, contain it. Policies were introduced such as cleaning the city pavements every four months. But the plague was extremely hard to contain and in 1575 Venice suffered 3,691 deaths in six months, a total that rose to 50,000 by June 1576 after a doctor from Padua had given the all clear. The Redentore on the island of Giudecca was subsequently built in the hope of divine intervention. But then came 1630.

From the Salute vaporetto stop head straight into the church of Santa Maria della Salute.

The impressive Santa Maria della Salute Church is built on the site of a monastery and church dedicated to the Holy Trinity. The land was donated by the Serenissima to the Order of the Knights Templars in payment for help received fighting the Genovese in 1256. Despite the disbanding of the order, the monastery remained until Pope Clemente VIII suppressed it and assigned it to the Republic in 1592. A wooden construction initially took its place, but during the plague of 1631 it was decided to build a more potent symbol to the Madonna to plead for an end to the epidemic. Designed by Baldassarre Longhena, the church of Santa Maria della Salute is a real wonder. Unfortunately, the Doge of the time did not live to see the building finished – he perished along with almost 50,000 other plague victims over the course of 1630.

2 From the church of Santa Maria della Salute turn right and walk through Campo della Salute, along Fondamenta Dogana alla Salute to Punta della Dogana and the Dogana di Mare.

Built in the 15th century, it was here that sea traders paid their taxes to the Republic. A second customs post was established near Rialto, but this was dedicated to trade from the terra firma, especially that arriving by river. The Dogana di Mare, built in the 17th century, consists of many warehouses behind a distinctive exterior. On the top of the building is a golden ball on which stands Lady Fortune.

3 Backtrack to Santa Maria della Salute and continue by walking left around the church into Fondamenta della Salute. From here, take the third

WHERE TO EAT

[O] **LINEA D'OMBRA,**
Dorsoduro 19, Ponte dell'Umiltà;
Tel: 041 241 1881.
In a spectacular setting with a canalside view of the Redentore Church on Giudecca, the restaurant serves fish with international wines. €€

[O] **AI GONDOLIERI,**
Dorsoduro 366, San Vio;
Tel: 041 528 6396.
One of the best restaurants in Venice, offering an alternative classic Venetian cuisine. It includes the vegetarian-based menu particularly appreciated by the gondoliers for its vitamin-packed, energizing qualities. €€€

[O] **CAFFE LA PISCINA,**
Dorsoduro 782, Fondamenta Zattere ai Gesuiti;
Tel: 041 241 3889.
The bar and restaurant of Pensione La Calcina has an outdoor terrace that looks out over the Giudecca canal. The refined dishes and style of cooking have been handed down through the generations. €€

65

DISTANCE 1.5 miles (2.4km)

ALLOW 2 hours

START Salute vaporetto stop by the church of Santa Maria della Salute

FINISH Fondamenta Zattere ai Gesuiti by the Zattere vaporetta stop

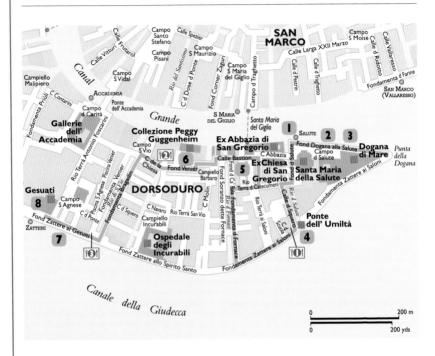

bridge leading to Rio Terrà dei Catecumeni and turn immediately left into Calle di Squero. Continue to the Ponte dell'Umiltà for a classic view of the Redentore on Giudecca.

Farther along the bank to the right is the home of the Reale Società Canottieri Bucintoro and museum. The association takes its name from the rowers of the *Bucintoro*, the fabulous golden craft used by the Doge during the annual Marriage of the Sea ceremony. The building was a symbol of Venetian maritime power. The *Bucintoro* was unceremoniously destroyed by Napoleon. The precious inlaid wood hull became a floating prison before being left to burn on the island of San Giorgio opposite the Riva.

REALE SOCIETÀ CANOTTIERI BUCINTORO;

www.bucintoro.org

4 From the Ponte dell'Umiltà turn right along Fondamenta Zattere ai Saloni, passing Calle Corte de le Scuola

and Rio Terrà ai Saloni on the right, to reach Fondamanta Fornace. Turn right into Fondamanta Fornace and follow Rio di Fornace. Make a right turn into Rio Terrà dei Catecumeni, and a left turn into Calle dei Morti and the church of San Giorgio.

The 11th-century former Benedictine abbey is adjacent to the church of San Gregorio and boasts a 14th-century door onto the Grand Canal. This is the spot where, in 899, during the governorship of Pietro Tribuno, a huge iron chain was stretched across the canal to stop the Hungarians attacking the heart of Venice.

The Hungarians were more feared than the Huns and the threat was such that a series of fortifications were constructed, leading all the way to the island of Olivolo. It was one of the first times Venice demonstrated its naval skills and determination to defend its territory.

5 Leaving the church, continue along Calle Bastion and over the bridge into Ramo Barbaro, then cross Calle Barbaro and keep right to the entrance of the Peggy Guggenheim Collection.

By all accounts Peggy Guggenheim (1898–1979) was an eccentric. Married to artist Max Ernst, her grave (which she shares with her 14 pet dogs, of which Cappuccino, Sir Herbert and Madam Butterfly were favourites) can be found in the exhibition gallery's grounds. As well as owning her own customized gondola, now in the Naval Museum, she bought one of Venice's most singular buildings to house her modern and contemporary art collection. This was the Palazzo Venier de Leoni, which had never been built higher than the ground floor possibly due to pressure from the neighbours who did not want to lose their view of the canal. The Leoni in the name is a reference to the Venier family's passion for keeping a lion on a lead – a fittingly eccentric place for Peggy's diverse collection.

COLLEZIONE PEGGY GUGGENHEIM;

www.guggenheim-venice.it

6 Exit the Peggy Guggenheim Collection from the garden gate

onto Fondamenta Venier dai Leoni and continue straight along Calle de la Chiesa. When the street opens into Campo San Vio, turn left into Fondamanta Bragadin, following this street to the Giudecca Canal and cross over the bridge at the end onto Fondamenta Zattere ai Gesuiti.

When syphilis broke out in the city in the 16th century, women were sent to the nearby Ospedale degli Incurabile, or Hospital of the Incurable, to be treated. The hospital was also an educational institute for their children, who were instructed in naval and maritime skills or given apprenticeships of particular use to the Republic. The building is now to become an extension of the Galleria dell'Accademia. On Fondamenta Zattere ai Gesuiti is a plaque marking the house where author John Ruskin (1819–1900) wrote *The Stones of Venice*, an epic of meticulous research. Even today it is considered the best and most detailed guide to Venice, capturing the soul of the city. He stayed here until 1877, writing his book between 1851 and 1852.

7 Go along Fondamenta Zattere ai Gesuiti to the church of Santa Maria del Rosario or Gesuati.

The Jesuits were expelled from Venice in a grave moral and religious crisis at the beginning of the 17th century, which once again pitted the city against the will of Rome. The Jesuits wanted to remain faithful to the Pope's wishes so they were duly escorted from the Republic for their own protection. As they filed away the populace shouted *Andaré in malora* (Go to the dogs); a cruel act as the Jesuits were a peaceful Order dedicated to work in the hospitals. Beside the church of the Jesuits is Campo Sant'Agnese, the place where the great plague of 1630 broke out. In front of the fountain, a house bearing an image of the Madonna marks the spot.

ASSOCIAZIONE CHIESE DI VENEZIA;
www.chorusvenezia.org

8 Either take the vaporetto to Giudecca over the canal or turn right to embark on Walk 23, 'Rising Tides and Watermarks'.

Where Marco Polo Grew up

A great walk to do at sunset when the canals are at their most beautiful and around every corner a gondola seems to glide silently by.

Marco Polo earned his immortality thanks to the book he wrote in prison in 1296 following his capture by Venice's great maritime rival, the Republic of Genoa. The book, entitled *Le Meraviglie del Mondo* is better known as *Il Milione*, the nickname given to Marco Polo. His father Niccolò had been known as *Il Milione Grande*. The family Polo had an established business in Constantinople and with the fall of the city in 1261 Niccolò transferred his interests to the Black Sea and further east. In his will of January 1323, Marco Polo asked to be buried in the church and monastery of San Lorenzo. Yet it was only in the 20th century that the exact location of the tomb was found, under the altar of San Sebastiano in the foundations of a previous church, adjacent to San Lorenzo. Today, it is part of an old people's home, but fittingly close to the modern Maritime Station, where the huge international cruise ships glide past to dock.

1 Starting in Campo Santi Apostoli, visit the church of Santi Apostoli.

The church of Santi Apostoli, one of the oldest in Venice, was named after the 12 apostles who appeared on this spot in the year 643 after a church was built in their honour. Above the canal bridge, looking out over Campo Santi Apostoli is the building where Doge Marino Falier lived. Falier has the ignominy of being the only Doge out of 73 to have his portrait blacked out in the Sala dei Maggior Consiglio in Palazzo Ducale. He was convicted of treason and beheaded in April 1355.

2 From Campo Santi Apostoli, cross over the small bridge through Sotoportego del Magazen, keeping left under the portico to reach Calle de le Magazen, which opens into Campiello Flaminio Corner. Cross over the bridge into Salizzada San Giovanni Crisostomo where the church of San Giovanni Crisostomo will appear on the left.

Near Campiello Flaminio Corner is a bidding house called Houshang Rachtian. Bidding houses thrived in medieval times when relics from Byzantium flooded into the Republic. Monks and religious experts would decide the value of the items and the bidding would start. Everyone wanted a valuable piece as a good luck charm. The bidding houses were also very popular following Napoleon's sack of the city, when many valuable treasures went under the hammer.

3 Exiting the church of San Giovanni Crisostomo, turn right and look for the clearly signposted Corte Prima dei Million o del Forno, Corte Secondo dei Milion and the small bridge over the Rio di San Lio.

No one knows exactly where the family home of Marco Polo was located, but it was certainly very close to the Corte Secondo dei Milion. Both the Corte Prima dei Million and Corte Secondo dei Million refer to the famous book written by the adventurer while being held captive by the Genovese. Marco's father and uncle had already ventured to the Orient and journeys lasting years were not unusual. The older men would typically return to Venice to take their sons off voyaging with them once they reached a certain age. Look out for the plaque on the wall of the Teatro Malibran that marks the likely location of the Polo's home.

4 Crossing the bridge, follow Calle Scaletta, turning left into Calle Dose, and then right into Calle Pindemonte, which opens into Campo di Santa Marina on the left.

Campo di Santa Marina marks the halfway point of this walk. Giacomo Casanova lived nearby in Palazzo Bragadin Carabba for nine years from 1746, the guest of his protector Matteo Giovanni Bragadin, who was a senator of the Republic. During a wedding ball 200 years earlier, earrings became a 'must have' fashion accessory for female nobility.

DISTANCE 1.5 miles (2.4km)

ALLOW 2 hours 30 minutes

START Campo Santi Apostoli

FINISH Campo Santi Apostoli

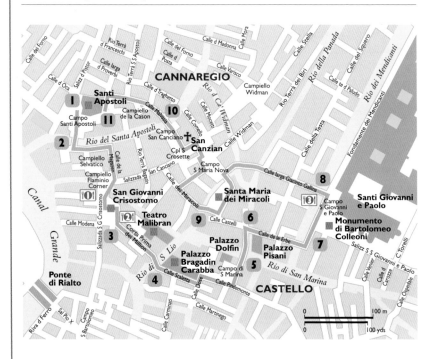

The trend was started in this palace, and the trendsetter was the wife of Giovanni Foscarini, who seems to have been inspired by the costumes of the Orient.

5 Leave Campo di Santa Marina by crossing the small bridge, which gives a fine view of both Palazzo Pisani and Palazzo Dolfin.

Giorgio Pisani was the famous Venetian *oratore* or ambassador to Rome at the time of the Cambrai League, an

allegiance between the Pope, France and Spain with the established aim of destroying Venice once and for all. Pisani is reported to have replied to the Pope's threat 'if the Pope wants to turn us back into the fishing village we once were, we will turn the Pontificate into the village parish it was once was'. Hearing this, Pope Julius II signed up for the Cambrai in 1508.

6 Walk straight ahead and take the first right into Calle de le Erbe and

WHERE TO EAT

🍴 FIASCHETTERIA TOSCANA,
Cannaregio 5719, S.Giovanni
Crisostomo;
Tel: 041 528 5281.
Despite its name the menu is strictly
Venetian, especially the fish, which
is caught from the lagoon or nearby
Adriatic Sea. €€€

🍴 HOTEL RISTORANTE PIZZERIA
MALIBRAN,
Cannaregio 5864, Corte del Teatro
Malibran;
Tel: 041 522 8028.
The restaurant of the hotel has a
270-degree view of the surrounding
streets and plenty of natural daylight
by which to enjoy classic Venetian
dishes and Veneto wines. €€

🍴 OSTERIA DA ALBERTO,
Cannaregio 5401, Calle Giacinto
Gallina;
Tel: 041 523 8153.
Small family-run osteria with a big
heart popular with Venetians. Typical
Venetian seafood dishes. The menu
is updated daily. €€

along to the Ponte Rosso. This marks the
border between the *sestiere* (district) of
Cannareggio and Castello and offers a
first and evocative glimpse of Campo
Santi Giovanni e Paolo.

The funeral services of the Doges were
held in the church of Campo Santi

Giovanni e Paolo and the church was
second only to St Mark's Basilica in
importance. It is a spectacular sight
and beautiful funeral urns and revered
monuments to many Doges, including
Tiepolo from 1249, Andrea Vendramin
from 1493 and Pietro Mocenigo from
1476 can be seen inside. Another famous
name connected with the church is
Marcantonio Bragadin; his mutilated
body was brought here following his
horrendous death at the hands of the
Turks in Famagosta. Not content
with cutting off his ears, drawing and
quartering, the Turks grimly stuffed his
body with straw and rode it around
town on an ox.

7 Enter Campo Santi Giovanni e
Paolo and stand beneath the statue
of Bartolomeo Colleoni.

The impressive statue in the middle of
the Campo Santi Giovanni e Paolo is
by sculptor Alessandro Leopardi, based
on designs by Verrocchio, a pupil of
Leonardo da Vinci. Leopardi's workshop
was in nearby Madonna dell'Orto. The
commission for the statue of Bartolomeo
Colleoni was troublesome from the
start. Having reluctantly inherited the
job following the death of Verrocchio,
Leopardi eventually finished the statue
but died prematurely of pneumonia
shortly after, cursing to the end.

8 Leave Campo Santi Giovanni e
Paolo by the bridge opposite the
church entrance. This leads into Calle
Larga Giacinto Gallina. Go ahead and

cross over two further bridges until you reach Campo Santo Maria Nova. Ponte Santa Maria Nova on the left leads to the church of Santa Maria dei Miracoli.

The church of Santa Maria dei Miracoli was reputedly built with donations left by passers-by at an image of the Madonna, which used to be located at this spot. The miraculous image now sits on the altar of the church, which was completed on New Year's Eve 1489.

9 Turn right after the church of Santa Maria dei Miracoli, crossing the bridge into Calle dei Miracoli. Take Campiello Bruno Crovato Gia San Canziani to get back into Campo Santa Maria Nova. Keep left and continue to the church of San Canzian or San Canciano.

Just over the bridge from Calle dei Miracoli is Calle de la Testa. The 'testa', or head, in question, is a piece of stone now fixed in the wall of a fairly modern building. It was here in the 15th century

that the Republic's executioner lived but did not work. The large head was much like a 'mouth of truth', into which were posted private messages to communicate the place and time of a probable execution. In other words, it was a memorandum for the executioner to keep the following day free.

10 Cross over the Ponte San Canzian into Calle della Malvasia. Keep left through Campiello de le Cason then Calle del Manganer to arrive back in Campo Santi Apostoli.

Not far from here is the narrowest *calle* in Venice. It is just 21in (53cm) wide and can be found at the end of Calle Varisoco. It beats two other narrow *calle* for the record by 2in (5cm).

11 Campo Santi Apostoli is a good spot to look for a restaurant and you can finish the walk with a drink in one of the traditional *osterie* along the Strada Nova.

TINTORETTO'S *THE CREATION OF THE ANIMALS* HANGS IN THE GALLERIE DELL'ACCADEMIA

The Last Gondola Maker

This walk is quite complicated and crosses the Grand Canal twice, but the interesting mix of ship-building yards and churches is worth the effort.

At the height of Venice's economic and political power, the most important industry of all was ship-building. As well as the huge commercial vessels that were built in the Arsenale, many smaller boats were built in *squeri* (boat-building yards) across the city. The various workshops located here also supported ancillary industries such as rope-making. The ropes were originally created from the reeds and plants of the Padana and the River Po plains. Many little boats were manufactured according to the job required: for example, the movement of cargo along the rivers was extremely important, bringing wood from Cadore and Belluno in the Veneto Dolomites. A list of types of boats includes *plati, sandoli, scaule, burchi* and, of course, the gondola. Once upon a time gondolas were painted in many different colours and were used for status and show, but a decree in 1633 democratically declared that all 10,000 of the vessels floating around the city should be painted black from that moment on. This tradition survives until the present day.

From the Zattere vaporetto stop pass by the Gesuati church on the left and continue along Rio Terrà Antonio Foscarini to the Church of S. Agnese.

The now filled-in Rio Terrà Foscarini canal is named after Antonio Foscarini, the Republic's ambassador to London in the first decade of the 17th century. A gregarious individual, he escaped punishment for suspected disloyalty.

2 Leave Campo S. Agnese and continue along Rio Terrà Antonio Foscarini. The Gallerie dell'Accademia looms large on the left and the entrance is located in Campo della Carità, at the foot of the Ponte dell'Accademia.

The Gallerie dell'Accademia was originally the Chiesa della Carità and Convent, an important *scuola* for assisting the poor. In the mid-16th century, Andrea Palladio received a commission to build a fine entrance hall and staircase. The oval stairway and tablinum were marvelled at by German poet Goethe (1749–1832) during his Grand Tour. Palladio's masterpiece was incorporated into the new gallery, which opened in 1807.

3 Cross over the Ponte dell'Accademia into Campo S. Vidal. Descending the steps into the *sestiere* (district) of San Marco, the building on the right is Palazzo Franchetti, now the Istituto Veneto di Scienze Lettere ed Arti. From Campo Vidal, continue into Campo Santo Stefano, passing the former church of S. Vidàl, now used as a concert venue.

WHERE TO EAT

⊙ RISTORANTE LA RIVISTA,
Dorsoduro 30123,
Rio Terrà Antonio Foscarini 979/a;
Tel: 041 240 1425.
The restaurant of the retro chic Ca' Pisani Hotel has its own entrance. Traditional Venetian dishes are revisited with a modern twist and the seasonal menus reflect the trendy ambience. €€€

⊙ VINERIA DAI DO CANCARI,
San Marco 3455,
Campo Santo Stefano;
Tel: 041 241 0634.
An elegant wine bar in the suitably named 'barrel street'. Inside, the wines are stacked in flagons and smaller casks to be tasted by the glass. €

⊙ OSTERIA AI ARTISTI,
Dorsoduro 1169/A,
Fondamanta della Toletta;
Tel: 041 523 8944.
A rustic and open location for breakfast or aperitif later in the day. Wine and food-tastings are organized in the evenings. €

In 1802 Campo Santo Stefano was the scene of a fatal accident, which put an end to public bull fighting performances in the city. On 22 February a stand full of helpless spectators collapsed, and this tragedy led to the authorities instigating a ban. In the centre of Campo Santo

79

DISTANCE **2 miles (3.2km)**

ALLOW **3 hours**

START **Fondamenta Zattere ai Gesuiti by the Zattere vaporetto stop**

FINISH **Ponte Lungo near the Zattere vaporetto stop**

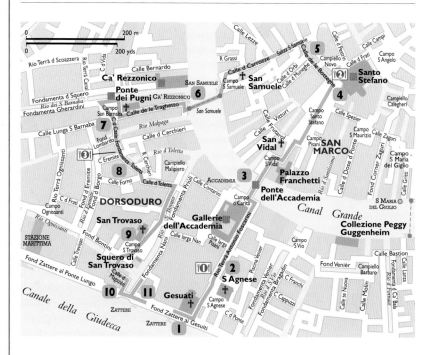

Stefano there is a statue dedicated to Nicolò Tommaseo who, along with Daniele Manin, guided a revolt against the Austrian rulers in 1848. The statue was erected in 1882.

4 Exit Campo S. Stefano at the top lefthand corner along Calle de le Botteghe. Before entering the calle, visit the Church of Santo Stefano.

The 13th-century Church of Santo Stefano is dedicated to St Stephen, the first Christian martyr. The church is also notable for the canal running under the altar. Known as the Rio del Santissimo, the canal runs all the way to the Ponte dell'Accademia and its course may be responsible for the visible lean of the bell tower. The tower was also hit by lightning in 1585, causing the bells to come tumbling down. Fortunately, however, they were replaced by four new ones, donated by Queen Elizabeth I following the dissolution of the Catholic churches and monasteries in England in the 1530s.

OPPOSITE: THE SANTO STEFANO BELL TOWER IS BUILT OVER A HIDDEN WATERWAY

5 Walk along Calle de le Botteghe. At the crossroads turn left into Salizzada San Samuele and continue along Calle de le Carrozze into Campo San Samuele and the crossing point over the Grand Canal.

Notice the shoes engraved on the stone column outside one of the shops along Salizzada San Samuele, No. 3126 to be precise. This indicated the house of a German cobbler who set up his business here. Stack heels were obviously the fashion. Today the shop sells carnival masks and costumes. The baroque Ca' Rezzonico palace on the other side of the canal is the home of the very fine museum of 18th-century Venice. It also boasts the largest ballroom in the city from the same period.

CA' REZZONICO;

www.museiciviciveneziani.it

6 Disembarking at Ca' Rezzonico continue along Calle de le Traghetto into Campo San Barnaba.

Just off Campo San Barnaba is the Ponte dei Pugni bridge. It was here that infamous fist fights between the black berets of San Nicolò dei Mendicoli and the red berets of Castello took place. The Castellani lived in the *sestiere* (district) of Castello, San Marco and Dorsoduro while the Nicolotti lived in Santa Croce, San Polo and Cannaregio. The antagonism was utilized by the Serenissima to keep future troops trim for battle and controlled skirmishes were encouraged elsewhere in the city from September to Christmas.

7 Leave Campo San Barnaba by Sotoportego del Casin dei Nobili and go over the Ponte Lombardo into Fondamenta della Toletta.

Not all the nobles of Venice were rich. Many branches of prestigious families found themselves in serious financial difficulty as the elite consolidated their power. The situation became so bad that almost 70 per cent needed assistance. Subsequently a law was passed that set aside state-subsidized accommodation in the district of San Barnaba. As a result, those nobles who moved there were given the nickname of 'Barnabotti'.

8 Follow Fondamenta Toletta into Calle della Toletta to the Rio S. Trovaso canal. Turn right before the bridge and walk ahead until you reach the church of San Trovaso on the right.

In 1779 a quarter of a body was fished out from the well in the main courtyard of the Church of San Trovaso by the local gondola-builder. A subsequent hunt for the remaining parts found the legs along Fondamenta del Malcanton and the head in Rio di Santa Chiara. The murder would have remained a mystery except for the initials on a paper roll used by the deceased to tie his hair. The trial led to the town of Este near Padova and the brother of the victim, Giovanni Cestonaro. He told how his brother had been suspicious for some time that his wife had been having an affair. And so it proved. The couple, Veneranda Porta and her lover Stefano Fantini of the Zattere, were beheaded and Fantini quartered like his victim. The house of Veneranda was demolished and the street renamed Calle della Madonna in the hope that such a horrid episode might be forgiven.

9 Exit the church into Campo San Trovaso. A small door on the left, just before the Ponte de la Scoasera, hides Venice's 'last' gondola maker.

There are a number of workshops where traditional gondolas are made and repaired, but the Squero di San Trovaso is the most visible and beautiful, and generations have been working in this spot for 300 years. A gondola today can fetch a price of 50,000 euros and the construction process of these boats is still a little secretive. The *'ferro'* is the classic decorative element on the prow. It is full of symbolic references to the city, from the curves in the shape of the Grand Canal to the seven comb-like teeth representing the six main districts of Venice and the island of Giudecca.
INSTITUTION FOR THE CONSERVATION OF THE GONDOLA; www.gondolavenezia.it

10 Cross over the Ponte de la Scoasera and follow Calle del Magazèn to Fondamenta Zattere. Cross over the Ponte Lungo bridge and walk 18m (20 yards) along Fondamenta Nani on the left for a wonderful view of the Squero di San Trovaso.

From Campo San Trovaso it is possible to peep into the workshop to see the

craftsmen at work, but to appreciate the setting and full activity of the Squero, the view from Fondamenta Nani is essential. During the time of the Republic, the craftsmen and raw materials needed to make gondolas typically came from the Cadore area of the Veneto Dolomites. Valuable tree trunks from the forest were floated down the Piave River to the lagoon to be used both for boat building and creating the traditional workshops.

11 The easiest way back to the centre of Venice is to turn left and walk along Fondamenta Zattere ai Gesuiti. Return to the Grand Canal by the Gallerie dell'Accademia and a suitable vaporetto.

ABOVE: *MADONNA WITH CHILD* BY BELLINI, GALLERIE DELL'ACCADEMIA

Charity, Fraternity and Great Art

A walk that takes you past a series of Venice's fine historical buildings containing much of the city's priceless art and history.

Confraternities (*scuole*) encouraged the development of art, religion and philanthropic life in Venice, as well as being places where people came together to help the needy. This walk passes two of the most important Confraternities – the Scuola Grande di San Giovanni Evangelista and the Scuola Grande di San Rocco. The other dominant *scuole* were S Teodoro, S Marco, Santa Maria della Misericordia and Santa Maria della Carità. Although the buildings we see today are magnificent, the splendour of Venice before the sack of the city by Napoleon can only be imagined. Numerous religious institutions supported by trade associations and benefactors saw their treasures taken. Thousands of sculptures, paintings and untold amounts of gold and silver were melted down into ingots and transported to Paris or Milan. Works by Carpaccio, Tiepolo, Bellini and Tintoretto were removed. One item that survives to this day in Venice, however, is the Pala d'Oro, an altarpiece in the Basilica San Marco. It was overlooked by the French, who underestimated its worth.

From Campo San Giacomo dell'Orio, leave the square by Calle de le Tintor. Go ahead and cross over the Ponte del Parrucchetta into Rio Terrà Parrucchetta until it reaches Rio Terrà Secondo. Turn right into Campo S. Agostin.

The area of Campo S. Agostin was home to one of Venice's liveliest new industries, typography. The value of the Guttenberg press was soon realized by the Serenissima and the Senate gave a concession to a German typographer. The first book, *Epistles of Cicero*, was published in 1469. Many entrepreneurs came to Venice to invest in the industry and further technical and typographical developments quickly followed, resulting in the creation of pocket books and other works. The first pocket Koran was printed in Venice.

2 Turn right out of Campo S. Agostin into Calle della Chiesa. Keep right towards Palazzo Giustinian and cross over the Ponte S. Agostin. Go ahead through Sotoportego de Pozzo Longo into Campiello Pozzo de Longo and continue to Calle de la Vida into Campo S. Stin. Exit the square by Calle de Tabacco and take the first right into Calle dell'Olio o del Cafetier. Pass under the arch on the first left into Campiello Scuola Grande di S. Giovanni Evangelista.

The Scuola of San Giovanni Evangelista was founded in 1261 but the building probably dates from the 5th century. Its Renaissance exterior was designed by Pietro Lombardo. The Gothic interior houses the reliquary of Santa Croce,

WHERE TO EAT

◙ PIZZERIA AE OCHE,
Santa Croce 1552, Rio Terrà Parrucchetta;
Tel: 041 524 1161.
Children will love this lively pizzeria named after three noisy geese. Choose from over 50 types of pizza, including the *Tuttoche* surprise pizza. €

◙ ANTICO CAPON,
Dorsoduro 3004, Campo S. Margherita;
Tel: 041 528 5252.
Located in the heart of this lively square, the Antica Capon serves a range of Mediterranean cuisine from typical Italian pizza to Spanish-style paella and scampi grills. €€

who gives the district its name. It was brought to Venice in 1369 by Philip Masser, who was chancellor of both Jerusalem and Cyprus at the time. At the end of the 14th century, during a procession of the Confraternity over the bridge to San Pietro in Castello, the heavy gold and jewelled case fell into the canal. Miraculously, it floated and was rescued. The powers of the relic were also noted during the French occupation, in particular during an inventory of the city's treasures. A functionary accidentally kicked the relic and suffered a mild injury which turned gangrenous. On his deathbed several days later he asked for pardon and removed the relic from

DISTANCE 2 miles (3.2km)

ALLOW 2 hours 45 minutes

START Campo San Giacomo dell'Orio

FINISH Ca' Rezzonico vaporetto stop

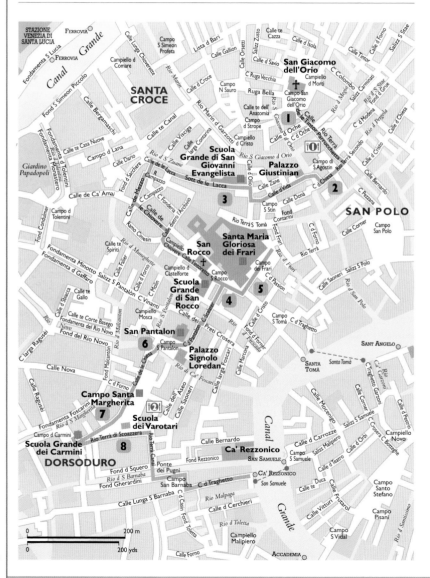

OPPOSITE: SANTA MARIA GLORIOSA DEI FRARI IS A UNESCO WORLD HERITAGE SITE

the list of treasures to be deported.
SAN GIOVANNI EVANGELISTA;
www.scuolasangiovanni.it

3 Leave Campiello Scuola Grande
di S. Giovanni Evangelista by
Sotoportego de le Lacca, which becomes
Calle de le Lacca. Before the bridge, turn
left into Calle de Mezzo, then go left at
the crossroads into Calle de le Chiovere.
Go ahead, keeping right into Campiello
de le Chiovere and Calle Tintoretto.

The splendid interior of the Scuola
Grande di San Rocco is decorated
with some of Tintoretto's finest works,
painted between 1564 and 1588. But the
choice of the artist was never a foregone
conclusion because, as with the Rialto
Bridge, the Serenissima had invited
competition for the contract to decorate
the interior of the building. All the
most famous artists of the time prepared
sketches and plans, but Tintoretto bribed
the porter to open up the *Scuola* so he
was able to take precise measurements.

He swiftly created a painting and hung it
in the space, declaring it a gift. According
to Venetian law a donation to any *scuola*
could not be refused. Who else could
finish the job?

4 From Campo San Rocco turn left
into Salizzada San Rocco and left
again, following the wall of the church of
Santa Maria Gloriosa dei Frari to the
entrance opposite the Ponte dei Frari.

It may seem like a long detour to enter
the church of Santa Maria Gloriosa dei
Frari and, in fact, the original building
was orientated in exactly the opposite
direction. Today's entrance is opposite
the Ponte dei Frari bridge, in a protected
zone. The church of Santa Maria Gloriosa
dei Frari took almost 160 years to build
and was finally consecrated in 1492. The
bell tower is 230ft (70m) high – only
St Mark's tower is taller – an whole-
hearted expression of Gothic Venetian
art. Among those who rest here are Doge
Francesco Foscari, Doge Benedetto
Pesaro, Claudio Monteverdi (1567–1643),
master of music for the chapel of St
Mark's, Titian (c1490–1576) and sculptor
Antonio Canova (1757–1822), whose
heart rests in a sombre white pyramid
built by his pupils. Look out for the State
Archives attached to the church by the
Ponte dei Frari where the original *Libro
d'Oro* or 'list of nobles' book is kept.
When Napoleon took over a copy was
ceremoniously burnt, along with other
symbols of Doge power.
ASSOCIAZIONE CHIESE DI VENEZIA;
www.chorusvenezia.org

ABOVE: INTRICATE STONEMASONRY ON THE EXTERIOR OF THE SCUOLA GRANDE DI SAN ROCCO

5 Backtrack to Campo San Rocco and take Sotoportego San Rocco on the left. Cross over the Ponte San Rocco into Calle Scalater and the island of San Pantalon. From Calle Scalater, take the first right into Calle d. Preti Crosera and then left into Calle San Pantalon, which curves right to the church of San Pantalon.

The church of San Pantalon is dedicated to St Pantaleon, a 4th-century physician from Asia Minor. It may still house a stone brought from Fort Mongioja in San Giovanni d'Acri by Lorenzo Tiepolo, commander of the Venetian fleet that defeated the Genovese in 1256. Before he left for battle he was told by the noble Signolo family 'if you defeat the Genovese, bring me back a stone from the foundations of the fort'. The stone was duly inserted into the corner of the church of San Pantalon, although it has since disappeared. Inside the church is the largest canvas painting in the world, created by Giovanni Antonio Fumiani (1645–1710). The work took 24 years to complete and is 466sq ft (433sq m) in size. Fumiani is buried here.

6 Cross over Rio di Ca' Foscari by the bridge in front of the church. Follow Calle de le Chiesa into Campo Santa Margherita.

Campo Santa Margherita is one of the few tree-lined squares in Venice and is one of the city's liveliest spots, both during the day and in the evening. The church of Santa Margherita is now used as a lecture hall by the University and is dedicated to St Margaret of Antioch. Her

cult was popular in Constantinople and a number of houses built in Byzantine style suggest the district was inhabited by merchants from Constantinople.

7 Walk the length of Campo Santa Margherita, passing the Scuola dei Varotari, dating from 1725, to the Scuola Grande del Carmini.

The *varotari* were leather workers or furriers who originally lived and worked in Campo dei Gesuiti. When they moved to Campo Santa Margherita, they took with them a marble relief of the Madonna, which had been attached to the exterior of the building. Near Campo dei Carmini is an old palace, once owned by the Moro family, known as the house of Othello. The plight of jealous owner Cristophoro Moro was celebrated in poetry in 1565, and later elaborated by Shakespeare in his famous play about the Moor of Venice. Moro's second wife was nicknamed *Demonio Bianco*, perhaps shortened by the bard to Desdemona. The Scuola Grande dei Carmini was designed by Baldassarre Longhena to house the Confraternity of the Carmelites and is dedicated to the Virgin Mary. Inside are nine works by Giambattista Tiepolo dating from 1739.

8 Finish by cutting through Campo Santa Margherita, exiting via Rio Terrà di Scoazzera before taking a right into Rio Terrà Canal and crossing over the Ponte dei Pugni. From Campo San Barnaba take Calle d. Traghetto to the Ca' Rezzonico vaporetto stop.

Tintoretto and the Northern Shore

An easy but bracing walk that compares and contrasts the daily life of modern Venetian residents with those of their ancestors.

This is one of the longest walks in the book, a sweeping route from Campo Santi Apostoli, a natural junction for Rialto, St Mark's Square and tourists heading on foot to and from Santa Lucia railway station. However, this walk will take you off the beaten track in the opposite direction to the Fondamenta Nuove that faces Murano, skirting the lagoon into the Cannaregio district of Venice. The focus is the great artist Tintoretto (1518–94) who lived and worked here, and whose name betrays the humble origins of a dyer. Many of the buildings visited on this walk have mysterious histories and improbable tales of ghosts, witches and spirits combined with stories of all-too-real tyrants. The walk passes the house of Tintoretto and the fabulous church of Madonna dell'Orto where he is buried. You will also meet three strange life-size characters who made this part of the city their base for trade and who have been immortalized in stone, a little satirically to say the least.

1 From Campo Santi Apostoli take Salizzada del Pistor, turning right into Calle Larga dei Proverbi.

Calle Larga dei Proverbi is a seemingly contradiction in terms. The *calle* are the alleys of Venice that are typically longer than they are wide. Calle Larga means a wide street, which is not what we see today.

2 Turn left into Rio Terrà SS Apostoli and go straight on, crossing Rio Terrà Barba Fruttarol into Salizzada L. Borgato. Cross the bridge onto Fondamenta dei Sartori and bear right into Salizzada Seriman. Cross over the bridge into Campo dei Gesuiti.

'Sartori' refers to the tailors or cloth-makers who lived and worked in this district. It was not just clothes they made, but also sails for ships. It must have been a tough life, and a hospital for impoverished workers once stood here. In stark contrast Palazzo Zen, built by Francesco Zen, is named after one of the Republic's most famous and adventurous merchant families. Carlo Zen became the hero of the Chioggia War when in 1380 with the might of his 18 ships, he saved the city from Genovese attack. His brothers Nicolò and Antonio also discovered Labrador in an expedition they themselves funded. The house we see today was once externally frescoed by Tintoretto.

3 Continue through Campo dei Gesuiti along Salizzada dei

WHERE TO EAT

🍽 **OSTERIA GIORGIONE,**
Cannaregio 4582,
Rio Terrà SS Apostoli;
Tel: 041 522 1725.
Dating from 1885, the *osteria* creates its daily menu from fresh fish chosen from the Rialto market and vegetables cultivated in small plots in the lagoon. €€

🍽 **A LA VECIA CAVANA,**
Cannaregio 4624, Rio Terrà SS Apostoli;
Tel: 041 528 7106.
A romantic spot for couples to enjoy a bottle of wine and an elegant meal in the atmosphere of an *enoteca* (wine bar/shop). €€

🍽 **AL FONTEGO DEI PESCATORI,**
Cannaregio 3711, Calle Priuli;
Tel: 041 520 0538.
Hidden away along the long Calle Priuli, this restaurant has a maritime atmosphere with fresh fish the order of the day. €€

Specchieri until you reach Fondamenta Nuove and the Tortuga bar and pizzeria. This is a great place to sit and enjoy the view of the lagoon.

Fondamenta Nuove was constructed in 1589 and it was intended that it would continue straight over the Sacca della Misericordia but this part of the project was never completed. It was along here that Casonova's mother lived.

OPPOSITE: THE VAULTED APSE OF THE 14TH-CENTURY CHURCH OF MADONNA DELL'ORTO

DISTANCE **2.5 miles (4km)**

ALLOW **3 hours**

START **Campo Santi Apostoli**

FINISH **Casa Tintoretto**

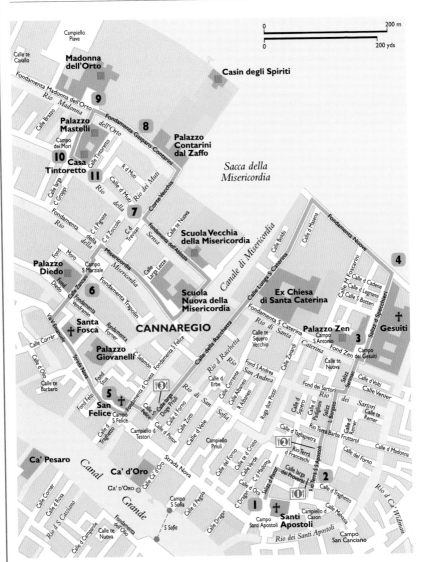

OPPOSITE: TINTORETTO WAS LAID TO REST IN 1594 IN THE CHURCH OF MADONNA DELL'ORTO

4 Walk along Fondamenta Nuove to the Sacca della Misericordia and the Canale di Misericordia. Turn left along Calle Lunga Santa Caterina, passing the former Chiesa di Santa Caterina. Continue along Calle della Racchetta over the Ponte Molin de le Rachetta and into Calle Larga Doge Priuli. At the end turn right into Calle San Felice and cross over the bridge into Fondamenta d. Chiesa. Turn left into Campo S. Felice.

The Calle Doge Priuli takes its name from one of Venice's noble families. Lorenzo Priuli became Doge in 1556 and his wife, Zilia Dandolo, was given a sumptuous pair of clogs to wear at the ceremony. Such occasions were used by trade associations to stimulate sales, both in the city and elsewhere. Another member of the family, Girolamo Priuli, became a well-known diarist.

5 Keep right after the church of San Felice and cross the wide bridge by Fondamenta Felzi. Continue on Strada Nova as it meets Via Vittorio Emanuele. At the church of Santa Fosca, turn right into Campo Santa Fosca and cross the bridge to Calle Zancani.

The nearby Palazzo Diedo was built by architect Andrea Tirali (1657–1737) whose soubriquet was 'the tyrant'. Having been sacked from a project by Francesco Grimani, he decided to irritate his former boss by building a more sumptuous building nearby. Infuriated, Grimani invited Tirali to view other projects, feigning he had changed his

mind about the sacking. Tirali was taken to a deserted point of the lagoon and forced to jump off at gun point. He obeyed and was rescued but humbled.

6 Cross over the Ponte Santa Fosca bridge into Campo S. Marziale. After a second bridge, turn right along Rio della Misericordia. Continue left along Fondamenta della Misericordia, passing the Scuola Nuova della Misericordia. Cross over the Rio della Sensa canal and turn left along Fondamenta dell'Abbazia, passing Scuola Vecchia della Misericordia.

The Scuola Vecchia Misericordia was built in 1310 and enlarged a number of times. What we see today dates from the 15th century. Two carved angels from a previous portal of the Scuola are in the Victoria and Albert Museum in London.

7 Take a right at the next bridge into Corte Vecchia. Continue until you reach Palazzo Contarini dal Zaffo.

Casin degli Spiriti, in the palazzo garden, was owned by the Contarini family and was a meeting place for artists and 'polite' society in the 1500s. Great artistic names as Sansovino, Titian, Giorgione and Pietro Aretino congregated here, and some say their presence still lingers in the air. When the Casin degli Spiriti was abandoned it became the location for legendary risqué parties and small boats filled with so-called witches departed from here to desert islands. Today it is a rest home for the elderly.

8 Follow Fondamenta Gasparo Contarini to Madonna dell'Orto.

Madonna dell'Orto takes its name from the orchard or garden that was tended here. Over 80 types of roses were cultivated, mainly for medicinal purposes. It was first known as the church of St Christopher after the patron saint of travellers, pilgrims and merchants until a statue of the Virgin Mary was unearthed in the garden. Tintoretto had a modest burial in the church in 1594 near to some of his finest works, notably the *Last Supper* and *Universal Justice*. His tombstone reads 'Jacobi Robusti – Tinctoretti'.

ASSOCIAZIONE CHIESE DI VENEZIA;

www.chorusvenezia.org

9 Leave Madonna dell'Orto by crossing the Ponte del Madonna dell'Orto bridge into Campo dei Mori.

Over to the left is Palazzo Mastelli, nicknamed Camel Palace. The palazzo was built by a family of 12th-century traders. Successful entrepreneurs from the Peloponnese (Morea, hence Mori), their commercial ties are clearly indicated by a relief of a camel on the exterior of the building canalside. The house was the base for three brothers who also feature in a less noble light a little further on in Campo dei Mori. In a reaction to their criticism of the Republic, they were unflatteringly represented in the petrified statues of Antonio Rioba, Alfani and Sandi carved into the corners of a building. A fourth, said to be their servant, is found nearer to Casa Tintoretto.

10 After Campo dei Mori, turn left before the small bridge and 14m (15 yards) on the left is Casa Tintoretto.

A modern doorbell indicates where Tintoretto lived and worked from June 1574 to 13 May 1594, the date of his death. The house has undergone many transformations and some say the building was constructed over an original convent, which later became an orphanage. Stories of small footprints in the snow in the internal garden persist, as well as tales about the eccentric character of the artist. Indeed, Tintoretto was fond of using a knife to take measurements for his portraits, often producing it without warning and terrifying his clients who understandably feared for their lives.

11 You can continue exploring this part of Venice by beginning Walk 5, 'The Ghetto Opens its Doors', at this point.

ABOVE: STATUE OF THE 'MOORS' SERVANT' OUTSIDE TINTORETTO'S HOUSE

The Maze from St Mark's Square to Rialto

This is an easy walk through the tumble of streets between St Mark's Square and Rialto, which is best undertaken in the early evening.

In the rush to get from the Rialto Bridge to St Mark's Square, or vice versa, it is easy to ignore the history of this district, now submerged by shops and tourists. There are many small areas and corners worth exploring. The walk is also suitable for visitors with disabilities, as there are a minimal number of bridges to cross and all those are equipped with wheelchair lifts. Starting from under the portico of the Correr Musuem, the route skirts Fondamenta Orseolo and the gondolas parked in the adjacent canal, to take in Calle dei Fabbri, chosen by Baiamonte Tiepolo as a route to storm the Palazzo Ducale in 1310 in an unsuccesful attempt to overthrow the Doge. A quick crossing of the Grand Canal to the area where the city's wine trade was based at the time of the Republic offers a waterborne view of the Rialto Bridge. The walk ends in the perfect location for an evening meal of traditional Venetian seafood pasta or an afternoon coffee, if you choose to take the walk earlier in the day.

1 From the Portico San Geminiano, the entrance to the Napoleon wing of the Museo Civico Correr, turn right into Calle Larga d. Ascensione. Continue ahead, passing Calle del Salvadego on the left, into Fondamenta Orseolo. Cross over the bridge into Calle Ungheria.

Salvadego is local dialect for 'wild' and was the name of an *osteria* that once stood in the *calle* of the same name. It seems to be a reference to Omo Salvadego, a legendary local man distinguished by a large black moustache, big hands and nose, eyes like cannon barrels and a mouth like a wood-burning oven.

2 Follow Calle Ungheria until it meets Calle dei Fuséri. Turn right and walk ahead until you reach Campo San Luca.

Campo San Luca is a popular meeting place, especially during Carnival. The more modern feel here is due to the dominance of the savings bank, Cassa di Risparmio di Venezia. The 1960s appearance of the building, by Luigi Nervi and Angelo Scattolin, was the result of a revival of traditional Venetian architecture using modern building materials and methods. Today, the ground floor hosts exhibitions and other cultural events. The bank was originally set up in 1822, in the former building, when it was based on the model of similar central European institutions in Vienna, Prague and Ljubljana.

3 Leave Campo San Luca by taking Calle del Magazèn, which runs into Calle dei Fabbri.

Calle dei Fabbri is the most direct route from Rialto to the heart of San Marco. About half way along it crosses Rio Terrà di Colonne. The name of the *rio* is the key to understanding how this district once looked. *Terà* (*terrà*) indicates that this was a canal subsequently filled in, while *colonne* means column in Italian.

4 Follow Calle dei Fabbri to the left in the direction of Rialto.

Calle dei Fabbri follows the route a group of insurgents took to overthrow the Doge on the 14 June 1310. The plot was hatched and led by the respected Baiamonte Tiepolo, who was looking to avenge past injustices against his family name. The plan was to march from the Pescheria zone of Rialto, where the house of another plotter, Querini, was located, and then proceed down Calle dei

DISTANCE I mile (1.6km)

ALLOW I hour 15 minutes

START Museo Civico Correr

FINISH Ponte di Rialto (Rialto Bridge)

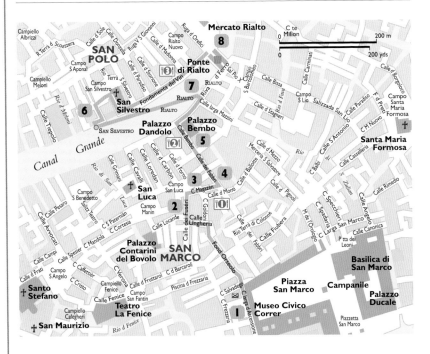

Fabbri to meet up with reinforcements arriving from Le Mercerie. So confident were they of the victory, their bragging alerted the officials of the Republic. The Doge's men dispersed the insurgents in and around Campo San Luca, forcing them back over the Rialto Bridge. The rebels set fire to the drawbridge to protect their backs. Querini died in the ensuing fracas and most of the insurgents were arrested, but Baiamonte Tiepolo somehow managed to get off lightly with a period of exile in Istria.

5 Keep straight ahead into Calle Bembo to Palazzo Bembo, which faces the Grand Canal. Turn right over the Ponte di Ferro bridge onto Riva del Ferro. Take the Rialto vaporetto across the Grand Canal to San Silvestro.

The urbanization of the district of San Silvestro dates from the turn of the first millennium. It was here that one of the city's first brick-built buildings was procured by the religious leader, the Patriarch of Grado. It was also here,

OPPOSITE: CHIESA DI SAN SILVESTRO

WHERE TO EAT

[101] LE BISTROT DE VENISE,
San Marco 4685, Calle del Fabbri;
Tel: 041 523 6651.
The dining rooms and the visible
kitchen make the elegant but informal
bistro a warm and welcoming
environment. It is a good choice
for lunch. €€

[102] ANTICA CARBONARA,
S. Marco 4648, Calle Bembo;
Tel: 041 522 5479.
The restaurant dates from the 18th
century when the coal merchants
would meet, drink and rest here. The
historic atmosphere is guaranteed as
the tables and alcoves are made from
the masts of a yacht belonging to the
son of a Habsburg emperor. €€

[103] TRATTORIA ALLA MADONNA,
San Polo 594, Calle d. Madonna;
Tel: 041 522 3824.
This bustling trattoria near the
Grand Canal, also popular with
local residents, has a friendly and
attentive service. The black squid is
recommended. €€

in 1177, that the Republic of Venice
first took a role in European diplomacy
by brokering a reconciliation between
Pope Alexander III (1105–1181) and
Frederick Barbarossa (1122–1190), the
Holy Roman Emperor. Preliminary
negotiations were held in San Silvestro
and four months later Barbarossa kissed

the Pope's feet and fondly embraced him,
finally signalling peace.

6 Leaving the vaporetto station turn
right, then left, followed by a right
turn into Campo San Silvestro. Head
back to the Grand Canal by passing the
right side of the church of San Silvestro
onto Fondamenta del Vin.

Fondamenta del Vin is named after
the wine imported here. As the trade
developed, the area expanded and by
the 17th century, nearby Campo San
Silvestro had become the central wine
trading point in Venice. Wine was
sold by the glass in St Mark's Square.
Itinerant sellers would stake their pitch
in the shade of the Campanile, moving

OPPOSITE: SHOPS LINE THE RIALTO BRIDGE

round to remain in the bell tower's shadow so their wine maintained an acceptable temperature. To this day, Venetians traditionally ask for a glass of *ombra* (shade) rather than a glass of wine.

ITALY FOOD, HISTORY AND CULTURE;

www.deliciousitaly.com

7 Go along Fondamenta del Vin to the Rialto Bridge.

The present Rialto Bridge is not the original. A previous wooden drawbridge, in existence from the 12th century, allowed large masted commercial vessels to navigate the Grand Canal. As the use of the canal changed, and after numerous collapses, a new bridge was commissioned in 1588. The work was put out to tender and all the great architects of the period competed for the influential contract, including the illustrious Palladio. The suitably named Antonio da Ponte (1512–1595) eventually won. Da Ponte's design was at first considered impossible and took some three years to build. The foundations comprised 10,000 wooden posts, inserted as supports for the stones of the bridge. Funds for the construction were raised through a public lottery.

8 The Rialto Bridge is the central point of the city. It may be too late in the day to visit the famous market, but consider taking the vaporetto back to St Mark's Square.

THE RIALTO BRIDGE STANDS AT THE HEART OF VENICE

Carlo Goldoni, Masks and Theatre

Take this walk to discover the 18th-century theatrical traditions of Venice, as seen through the eyes of playwright and author Carlo Goldoni.

Carlo Goldoni was born in Venice in 1707, his lifetime spanning the last and most tumultuous century of the Republic. This period was also the age of the Grand Tour, when young men came from around Europe to experience the art and culture of Italy. Goldoni documented the life and people of the time in theatrical form, and by using satire and grotesque characters in his writing, he was able to comment on the decline and excesses of a society already politically and economically corrupt. His writing paved the way for modern theatre, no longer using the traditional 'Commedia dell'Arte' method of writing. Goldoni was a contemporary of notables such as the outstanding composer Vivaldi and the notorious womanizer Casanova, He died in Paris in 1793, less than five years before the Republic fell. He would have viewed the fall as the greatest of all tragedies that not even a carnival mask could hide. As you walk you will find that many of the names of streets and alleys have theatrical references.

1 Facing Fondaco dei Tedeschi, the home of the present day post office, turn left into Campo S. Bartolomeo.

The superb statue of Goldoni in the square is a fitting tribute to the great protagonist of 18th-century theatre. Created by Antonio dal Zotto almost a century after the playwright's death, it is considered one of his best works. In 1907 a bronze scroll and theatre mask were added to enhance a proud Goldoni in clothing typical of the period. Note his plays poking out of his pocket.

2 Leave Campo S. Bartolomeo along Via 2 Aprile and pass the Scuola Grande di San Teodoro on the right. Continue along Calle d'Ovo and over the Ponte d'Ovo into Campo del Teatro o de le Commedia.

Behind the church of San Salvador is the spot where the great fire of 1492 miraculously came to a halt. It had broken out near the Spaderia (sword workshops), close to Santa Maria Formosa, and spread with such speed towards Rialto that its destructive path seemed unstoppable. Yet it did stop, and in dramatic fashion. A wall statue of the Madonna and the infant Jesus marks the precise location. Teatro Goldoni dates from the early 17th century and was once known as Teatro San Salvador.

3 Turn right after Teatro Goldoni into Corte del Teatro, then first left towards Calle del Carbon, and then right to Riva del Carbon.

Riva del Carbon was the only place in Venice where coal could be unloaded. A plaque near the entrance to Palazzo Farsetti, along the Grand Canal, commemorates the people of Venice for their courage in liberating the city during the World War II, and for saving Venice from any real damage. The words, in Italian, are those of US General Mark Clark from 3 May 1945.

4 Turn left along Riva del Carbon to the front of Palazzo Farsetti and Palazzo Loredan.

Palazzo Loredan, also known as Ca' Loredan, originally belonged to the noble Corner family. It was here that Elena Lucrezia Corner Piscopia was born. She was the first ever woman graduate, gaining a degree in philosophy in 1678. Elena was the fruit of the scandalous marriage of her father Giovanni and a commoner, Zanetta Boni. Owing to this

DISTANCE **2.5 miles (4km)**

ALLOW **3 hours 15 minutes**

START **Post Office near Ponte di Rialto (Rialto Bridge)**

FINISH **Museo Casa Carlo Goldoni**

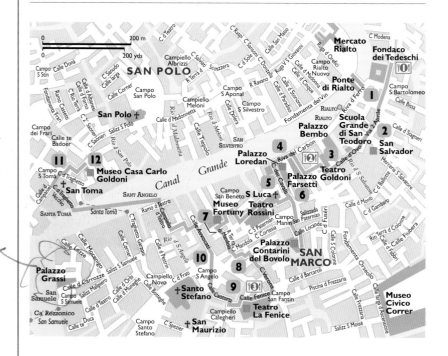

dubious parentage, Elena's original wish to study theology was denied, so she settled for a dissertation on Aristotle.

5 Turn away from the Grand Canal along Calle dei Cavalli.

It is worth making a slight extension through Campo Manin to discover Palazzo Contarini del Bovolo, one of Venice's most striking sights. It is renowned for its Renaissance tower, attached to the outside of the Palazzo.

Within the tower is a spiral staircase. Local legend has it that the staircase was built by Giovani Candi in 1499 to allow Pietro Contarini to reach his bedroom on horseback. The Bovolo refers to the type of staircase, but its prominence and popularity soon became attached to the residence of the Contarini.

6 From Calle dei Cavalli follow Ramo a Fianco la Chiesa to the church of San Luca. Cross over the Ponte dei Teatro at the entrance to the Corte

OPPOSITE: THE MAGNIFICENT STAIRCASE OF CONTARINI DEL BOVOLO PALACE

d'Appello and follow Calle de le Muneghe around Teatro Rossini to reach Salizzada de la Chiesa o de Teatro. Continue to Campo San Beneto and the Museo Fortuny.

The 14th-century palazzo, now home of the Fortuny Museum, was built by the Pesaro family, who subsequently moved to a new prestigious palazzo, the Ca' Pesaro on the Grand Canal. At first, their former home became a music college, before being bought by the eclectic Spanish artist Mariano Fortuny Y Madrazo (1838–1874). On his death it was left to the Comune di Venezia for the benefit of the people of the city.
MUSEO FORTUNY;
www.museiciviciveneziani.it

7 Exit the Museo Fortuny and turn right, then right again, into Remo Orfei, then left into Rio Terrà di Mandola. Continue straight ahead, crossing Calle della Mandola into Rio Terrà dei Assassini.

Before Venice had any form of street lighting, dead bodies were often found in this district. Such was the worry over crime, the Serenissima established the figure of the *codega*, a sort of night watchman. In 1732 street lighting was introduced across the city.

8 The twisty Rio Terrà dei Assassini meets Calle della Verona and turns right to continue to Campo San Fantin and the Teatro La Fenice.

La Fenice theatre has burned down twice – in 1836 and in 1996. On both occasions, as its name suggests, the theatre was reborn out of the flames, just like a phoenix (*fenice*). The 1996 fire was the most devastating and all that remained were the outside walls. La Fenice was the first theatre in Venice to be constructed with a dedicated entrance. Previously, most theatres were converted rooms in palaces. Closed from 1996 until 2003 for refurbishment, the theatre once again produces fine operatic performances.
TEATRO LA FENICE;
www.teatrolafenice.it

9 Leave Campo San Fantin by Calle della Fenice to the right of the theatre door. Passing Campiello Fenice on the right go ahead, following the Sottoportico and over the Ponte Storto to Calle Caotorta and Campo Sant'Angelo.

The Istituto Poligrafico e Zecca dello Stato (or mint) can trace its history to the Venetian monetary system that was instigated in 1284, after the collapse of the Byzantium coinage. As well as silver pieces the mint produced the gold *ducato* or *zecchino*. At one point the Republic was earning ten million *zecchini* from exports.

10 Leave Campo Sant'Angelo by Calle degli Avvocati. Take the first left turn over the small bridge and into Calle dell'Albero, which becomes Campiello del Teatro, meeting Ramo del Teatro at the Grand Canal. Take the Sant'Angelo *traghetto* for one stop to Santa Tomà. Leave the vaporetto stop and go along Calle del Traghetto Vecchio to Campo San Tomà.

Campo San Tomà is a fine artisan theatrical mask shop and workshop, situated to the right of the square as you look at the church of San Tomà from the middle of the campo. The shop is called 'Sole Luna' and when you walk in you can feel an atmosphere redolent of costume and the theatre. All the masks are made of papier mâché, just as they were at the time of Goldoni.

11 Turn right in front of the church of San Tomà and continue straight to cross over the bridge to the Museo Casa Carlo Goldoni.

This small museum is housed in the Ca' Centani building where Goldoni spent the first part of his life. A collection of marionettes is displayed along the walls and there is a miniature theatre, used for entertaining children. The museum also houses a library of 30,000 specialist books

WHERE TO EAT

[O] **BACARO JAZZ,**
San Marco 5546, near Campo San Bartolomeo;
Tel: 041 528 5249.
Lively restaurant and cocktail bar close to the Rialto Bridge, with a jazz theme and live music. €

[O] **ANDREA ZANIN BAR,**
San Marco 4589, Campo San Luca;
Tel: 041 956 369.
A trendy cake shop and counter service offering light snacks, drinks and delicious cakes, managed by a firm of well-known caterers. €

[O] **RISTORANTE TAVERNA LA FENICE,**
San Marco 1939, Calle Fenice;
Tel: 041 522 3856.
Anyone who is anyone has eaten at this elegant restaurant beside the famous theatre. Dress up for a refined fish-based menu. €€€

and a theatre study centre. Of particular interest is an interactive map with colour-coded wooden bricks that locates all the theatres in the city where Goldoni's plays were performed.
MUSEO CASA CARLO GOLDONI;
www.museicivicivenezani.it

12 Finish by heading back to the Santa Tomà vaporetto or proceed along Walk 21, 'Artisans of Venice', which starts here.

Stories between Three Museums

This walk is a logical extension to an early visit to the Rialto market and ends in Campo San Giacomo dell'Orio, a suitable spot for lunch.

From the sacred to the profane, this walk contrasts various aspects of Venetian society and daily life, taking as reference points three fabulous palaces that are now interesting museums. The first encountered is Palazzo Ca' Pesaro, which exhibits both modern art and oriental artefacts. The second is the Natural History Museum, situated in the Fondaco dei Turchi, a former base for the Turkish traders in the city. Between the two is the Museo del Tessuto e del Costume (Museum of Textiles and Costumes), located in Palazzo Mocenigo. It has a fine collection of textiles and related information. Here, too, the museum demonstrates the daily life of a noble family through a series of original rooms, from reception areas for greeting important guests to the bathroom of the lady of the house. High-class prostitutes operated in this district and have clearly left their mark in the names of local bridges.

1 Leave Campo S. Aponal by Calle del Ponte Storto. Cross over the Ponte Storto into Calle Salviati, which opens into Campiello Albrizzi.

The *cortigiane* (courtesans or upper-class prostitutes) were perhaps not the first examples of the modern emancipated woman, but they certainly were worthy of a gentleman's attention from the 16th century through to the time of the Grand Tour. To differentiate themselves from common prostitutes their independence allowed them the luxury of only sleeping with whom they liked. A *cortigiana* had to be courted, wooed and won over, but the career was only open to the very beautiful and particularly cultured. A guide was printed in 1570, the *Catalogue of all the Principle and Most Honourable Cortigiane of Venice*, in which 215 ladies were listed with price indications for those who wanted an introduction.

2 Take a right at Calle Albrizzi, which leads to Rio Terrà Carampani, Fondamenta de la Stua and Rio di S. Cassiano.

In the 14th century the Serenissima tried to contain prostitution within the city in a series of houses called *castelli*. The aim was not only to control the business that had always flourished but to actively promote heterosexuality, so countering the trend of homosexual behaviour among young males. The girls were asked to flaunt their bodies at every opportunity. The infamous Ponte de le Tette takes its name from a part of their anatomy displayed by

prostitutes in all weathers. The alternative for young men, who refused such temptations and pursued homosexuality, was a capital sentence between the twin columns in St Mark's Square.

3 Having crossed Ponte de le Tette follow Calle dell'Agnello and take the first right turn into Fondamenta Agnello. Go ahead to Calle della Regina and turn right. Follow Calle della Regina taking a right into Sotoportego de Siora Bettina and over the Ponte de le Chiesa bridge into Campo S. Cassiano.

The old theatre of San Cassiano or San Canzian was the first theatre to sell tickets, in 1637, for a peformance of musical opera, meaning that anyone who could afford to buy one could attend. Prior to this, audiences of such spectacles had been invited members of the nobility. The performance was *Andromeda* by Francesco Manelli (1594–1667).

DISTANCE 1.5 miles (2.4km)

ALLOW 3 hours

START Campo S. Aponal in the Rialto district

FINISH Campo San Giacomo dell'Orio

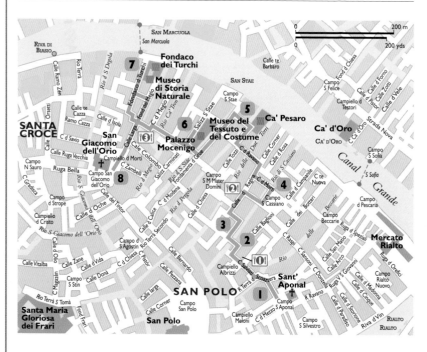

4 Leave S. Cassiano by the second bridge over Rio di S. Cassiano leading to Calle dei Morti and rejoining Calle della Regina. Turn right, and then first left, into Campo del Ravano. Cross over the bridge and take the first right to Ca' Pesaro.

Palazzo Ca' Pesaro, completed by the end of the 17th century, is a fine example of Venetian baroque architecture. Today it houses the collection of modern art bought, in the main, by the Venice

municipality during the many Biennale Art exhibitions of the 20th century. The second floor is dedicated to oriental art.

CA' PESARO;

www.museicivicivenezivani.it

5 Backtrack from Ca' Pesaro to cross over the Ponte Pesaro on the right into Calle Pesaro. Turn left into Fondamenta Rimpetto Mocenigo until you reach Campiello del Spezier and then over the Ponte de la Rioda on the right into Salizzada S. Stae.

OPPOSITE: CA' PESARO IS VENETIAN BAROQUE AT ITS FINEST

Palazzo Mocenigo houses the Museo del Tessuto e del Costume. Here you can learn about 'point lace', a 16th-century invention, also known as *punto in aria* or 'stitch in the air', which allows lace creations without textile support. The Mocenigo family provided the Serenissima with seven doges, from Tommaso (1414-1423) to Alvise IV (1763-1778), and a Mocenigo was also the Republic's ambassador to London. For all their nobility, the room that stands out the most is the bathroom (and its plumbing) of the lady of the house, dating from the early 20th century.

PALAZZO MOCENIGO;

www.museicivicivenezia.it

6 Exit Palazzo Mocenigo and then backtrack to Calle del Tintor. Make a right turn and cross the Ponte del Tintor. Keep left and cross over the Ponte dei Megio into Fondamenta del Megio on the right. A left turn brings you to Fondaco dei Turchi.

The Fondaco dei Turchi was built in the 13th century as a luxurious residence for the Pesaro family. It was so plush it was often used to entertain royalty. It had a series of owners before being rented from the Republic by the Turkish community. This was as much to keep an eye on the Turks as to offer them a base for trade and warehousing. Near here is another old warehouse called Fontego del Megio. Dating from the 14th century, it was a granary store where millet of dubious quality or forage – food considered only suitable for cattle or horses – was kept

for emergencies. It took a lot to feed a city with the third largest population in Europe after Naples and Paris, and with no land to grow grain. Nevertheless, such was the roughness of the bread made from the grain that even during a period of plague those who received it as rations complained that it was killing more people than the actual disease. It was so bad not even dogs or cats would touch it.

7 Backtrack along Fondaco dei Turchi and carry on to Calle de Spezier, reached after a couple of twists at the Ponte dei Megio. Go along Calle Larga to Campo San Giacomo dell'Orio.

The Natural History Museum, along Fondaco dei Turchi, houses the impressive dinosaur finds of palaeontologist Giancarlo Ligabue following his expedition to Niger in 1973. The giant 39ft (12m) flesh-eating crocodile may not have frequented the Venetian lagoon, but the aquarium on the ground floor gives an idea of the environment of the lagoon, and in particular the reefs situated off the Venetian coast, which sustain a rich fauna. At the same time as the museum was formed, a library was created for researchers and specialists in the field of natural history. The name Campo San Giacomo dell'Orio is said to derive from either the laurel plants that grew here or the original *luprio* or marshland. Whatever the truth, the church of San Giacomo dell'Orio dates from the 9th century and is the only surviving example of integral Venetian-Byzantine architecture. In the *campo* is the old seat

WHERE TO EAT

[O] TRATTORIA ANTICHE CARAMPANE,
San Polo 1911, Rio Terrà Rampani;
Tel: 041 524 0165.
This well-known restaurant with a relaxed atmosphere is situated in a quiet square. It is popular with politicians and celebrities. €€

[O] OSTERIA VECIO FRITOLIN,
Santa Croce 2262, Calle della Regina;
Tel: 041 522 2881.
Fritolin were places where fish was fried on large open grills until the practice was stopped in the last century for fear of fire. This restaurant is a lasting monument to the delicacy. €€

[O] OSTERIA LA ZUCCA,
Santa Croce 1762, Calle del Tintor;
Tel: 041 524 1570.
Overlooking a small canal in a very picturesque spot, La Zucca serves creative dishes and is a good lunchtime choice, especially for vegetarians. €

of the Collegio dei Medici Fisici, dating from 1671.
MUSEO DI STORIA NATURALE;
www.msn.ve.it

8 The walk reaches its conclusion with Walk 12, 'Charity, Fraternity and Great Art', beginning from Campo San Giacomo dell'Orio.

THE STUNNING FONDACO DEI TURCHI

Contemporary Gardens to Ancient Castles

A longer walk in a wide-open district of the city, best done in the early morning. It would also make a good jogging route for the late afternoon.

This walk encompasses the history of Venice from its earliest inhabitants to the most modern of contemporary art exhibitions, La Biennale di Venezia. When the Biennale is not taking place, this corner of the city is extremely quiet and the tourist population is at an absolute minimum. It is not difficult to appreciate the way of life of the lagoon in former times by exploring the old Castello quarter, taking in the harbour, boatyards and housing toward the island of Olivolo, all of which are virtually unchanged since the 1800s. Despite the area being somewhat of a backwater, the local church of San Pietro di Castello is one of the most significant religious buildings in Venice and was the principal church of the Patriarch for almost the entire duration of the Republic. The house of the 15th-century explorer and mariner John Cabot, with its ship-like structure, fittingly concludes the walk.

From Campo San Biagio, opposite the Naval Museum, turn left on Riva San Biagio. Cross over the Ponte de la Veneta Marina o de le Cadene and along Riva dei Sette Martiri. Continue to the Giardini vaporetto stop, opposite the Giardini Pubblici in Viale dei Giardini Pubblici.

This long and beautiful promenade was completed in 1937 and in effect linked Piazza San Marco to the public gardens of the Biennale zone. The name Riva dei Sette Martiri refers to the seven partisans shot under the fascist rule; it was previously called Riva dell'Impero in honour of Mussolini. The gardens are also known as Giardini Napoleonici or Napoleonic Gardens, created following the clamorous French occupation at the end of the 18th century by draining an area of marshland. Their construction resulted in the demolition of a large part of the city and some churches, including San Dominco di Castello, as well as a ducal annexe. Only a few of the great treasures from the churches were saved and are now on display in the Gallerie dell'Accademia. The gardens are well-known for the many cats that run wild in the vicinity.

2 Take a left into Viale Trieste, which leads to the Biennale.

Some hundred years after the creation of the public gardens, poet Riccardo Selvatico and art critic and mayor Antonio Fradeletto proposed the Biennale as a contemporary art exhibition. Princess Elizabeth 'Sissi' of

WHERE TO EAT

🍽 HOSTARIA DA FRANZ,
Castello 754, Fondamenta San Giuseppe;
Tel: 041 522 0861.
This *osteria* attracts famous names from around the world from Monica Bellucci to Nicolas Cage. Its excellent fish dishes are still prepared using traditional Venetian recipes. €€

🍽 IL NUOVO GALEON,
Castello 1308, Via Garibaldi;
Tel: 041 520 4656.
The menu follows the seasons, the chef using local produce to create daily specialities. The Nuovo Galeon is part of the Buon Accoglienza Restaurant Association. €€€

🍽 OSTERIA AL GARANGHELO,
Castello 1621, Via Garibaldi;
Tel: 041 520 4967.
Run by two Venetian brothers, Lucio and Simone, the osteria serves genuine, traditional Venetian dishes from early morning until the late evening. €€

Austria was one of the visitors to the first International Exhibition of Art in 1895. She is reported to have been attracted to a painting featuring five naked women, whose modesty was concealed by various roses. 'For sure there are a few too many flowers' was her observation. The exhibition caused considerable controversy and the Patriarch called for Catholics to boycott the event.

DISTANCE 3 miles (4.8km)

ALLOW 2 hours 30 minutes

START Museo Storico Navale (Naval Museum)

FINISH Museo Storico Navale (Naval Museum)

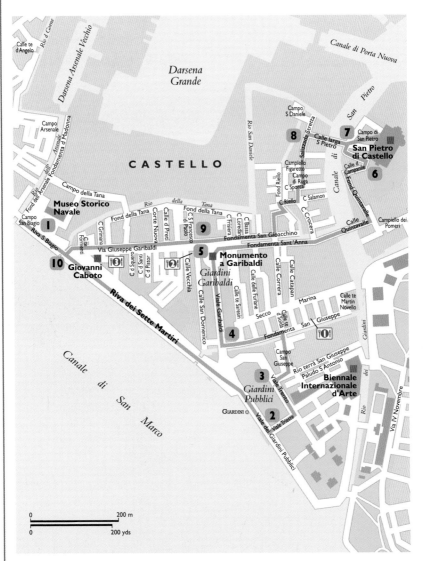

OPPOSITE: GARIBALDI'S MONUMENT STANDS IN ONE OF VENICE'S LEAST VISITED BUT INTERESTING DISTRICTS

The concept was ahead of its time and it wasn't until 1924 that Impressionist paintings were permitted to be displayed.

LA BIENNALE DI VENEZIA;

www.labiennale.org

3 Follow Viale Trento to an arched gate in the wall. Go through and turn left into Campo San Giuseppe. Walk ahead, and cross over the Ponte S. Isepo, then left onto Fondamenta San Giuseppe.

The arch on the left, known as the Arco di San Michele, dates from the 16th century and is the only remaining part of the church of S.Antonio Abate, which had been demolished on the orders of Napoleon. Look carefully and you can see the original steps to the canal where the boats would moor.

4 Cut through into Viale Garibaldi, continuing to the end to see the statue of the famous Italian hero.

The monument to Guiseppe Garibaldi (1807–82) has been fittingly placed in front of the widest street in Venice. The boulevard was not originally built to honour Garibaldi, but by Napoleon who had a passion for large boulevards in which to promenade his troops.

5 Turn right along Fondamenta Sant'Anna and cross the Ponte de Quintale bridge, which leads onto the Island of S. Pietro di Castello and into Calle Quintavalle. Turn left into Fondamenta Quintavalle. Continue, taking a right turn into Calle dietro il Campanile.

The island of San Pietro di Castello was home to one of the first communities in the lagoon to establish a permanent base. The island was called Olivolo, most likely due to the presence of the many olive trees cultivated here, but possibly because of its shape. What began as a base for a small fort expanded to form the city's largest *sestiere* (district). According to Humanist and writer Tito Livio, this castle was built by the Eneti people as their extreme northern Adriatic base. It is more probable the fortifications were built by Doge Pietro Tribuno in 906, to defend the city from the Tartars who knew how to construct and use good, seaworthy boats and were capable of launching an invasion on the city.

6 Leaving Calle dietro il Campanile, Campo S. Pietro and the church of San Pietro di Castello come into view.

The church of San Pietro di Castello was the seat of Venice's Patriarch until Napoleon transferred all municipal powers to Palazzo Ducale. The dome of the church is only 13ft (4m) lower than that of St Peter's in Rome. Inside the church is a stone throne, allegedly used by St Peter in Antioch. The backrest is formed from an old Muslim tombstone, complete with Arabic writing, while the seat probably dates from the 13th century.

7 Leave Campo S. Pietro by crossing the Ponte di San Pietro.

The *campo* opposite the church is one of the few not paved. Here you will find simple grass, earth and trees. If you look closey between the church and the bridge it is possible to see a white rectangular stone; it was here the Doge and Patriarch would meet formally. It was a neutral spot equidistant from the threshold of the church and the mainland of Venice, a place to pay their respects to each other. Immediately after the bridge, note how the low windows of the buildings have been half blocked with concrete, a reminder of how much water penetrates the city.

8 Leave the bridge behind and follow along Calle larga di S. Pietro. Turn left into Salizzada Stretta and continue to Campiello Figaretto, which leads into Campo di Ruga. Continue by keeping right and then take a right turn into Calle Riello and over the Ponte Riello. An immediate left, then first right, leads into Calle San Gioacchino and Fondamenta. S. Gioacchino. Continue to Garibaldi's monument and Via Guiseppe Garibaldi.

The whole area leading back to the Naval Museum and Arsenale was dedicated to fishing and marine activity. Through the narrowest of *calle* on the right are spaces where the nets were hung out to dry and repairs made; ropes were made in Fondamenta della Tana. Shop fronts in this area typify the maritime theme, a far cry from the bustle of tourism of central Venice. For example, the window of the Society of Carpenters and Caulkers is full of wooden toy boats and classic boat making tools. Other signs

include a plaque indicating the correct measurement for selling fish.

9 Via G. Garibaldi ends in a curious wedge shape. The final building is the house of explorer, Giovanni Caboto, more commonly known as John Cabot (c1450–c1500).

What is distinctive about the house is its shape. It reaches along the street straight towards the Giudecca Canal and gives the impression of a bow of a ship looking out to sea, or to the horizon. A plaque on the wall tells us more. John was in the pay of the English to open up new commercial routes, such as the North West passage. He went on to discover Newfoundland and Canada and famously planted both the English and Republic of Venice flags.

10 The route finishes where it started, and it is possible to take a gentle stroll by the Canale di San Marco to St Mark's Square.

125

Terra Firma and Terra Veneta

A walk along the part of Venice closest to the Italian mainland and through a district that embodies the past, while looking to the future.

The Republic of Venice had a particularly boisterous relationship with the Veneto mainland during its history. Having left terra firma behind to forge its own identity, the success of the enterprise forced the Serenissima to look back to the mainland, as both a permanent food supply and to consolidate its power base closer to home following frequent attacks from across the Mediterranean. Yet it was only at the beginning of the 15th century that the Republic set serious eyes on incorporating the land into its political sphere. Verona, Vicenza, Padova, Rovigo, Treviso and Belluno were the first to fall under its control. The reign eventually extended to Bergamo, Brescia, Crema, Rovereto and Ravenna. By far the greatest gift to us all from this marriage of terra firma and terra Veneta was the surge of interest in fine art, and the influx of the great Tuscan and other artists who joined their Venetian contemporaries throughout the 1400s and beyond.

From the Ponte dei Tre Archi walk ahead to the church of San Giobbe in Campo San Giobbe.

During the 16th century Venice was at its most splendid, but not everyone was able to share the full benefits of the economic and social boom. The situation was made worse by famine and the increase in grain prices. In 1527, during a visit to the church of San Giobbe in Cannaregio by Doge Gritti, the crowd took the opportunity to vent their full frustration. Surrounding him they shouted '*abundantia abundantia*', demanding more food. The overlooked church of San Giobbe is the work of Pietro Lombardo and represents one of the first examples of Renaissance architecture in Venice, incorporating distinctive Tuscan influences.

ASSOCIAZIONE CHIESE DI VENEZIA;

www.chorusvenezia.org

2 Backtrack from the grounds of the church of San Giobbe towards the Ponte dei Tre Archi and turn right into Fondamenta San Giobbe, which extends into Fondamenta Savorgnàn and Fondamenta Venier.

The *sestiere* (district) of Cannaregio may derive its name from a derivative of Canal Regio (Royal Canal), a direct reference to the importance this waterway had as a thoroughfare to the mainland. It seems just as likely, however, that the root of the first syllable is taken from *canneti*, the reed beds once thick in this district.

3 Continue ahead, passing Palazzo Savorgnan and Palazzo Venier on the right, to reach the Ponte di Guglie. Turn left into Salizzada San Geremia and into Campo San Geremia.

Palazzo Labia is the headquarters of RAI, Italy's national television company, who have restored it and are now offering it for sale – but it has to be kept for cultural use. The building was one of Venice's finest noble houses and is named after the Labia family. They were extremely wealthy, having the interiors of the palazzo frescoed by Tiepolo, which

127

DISTANCE 1.5 miles (2.4km)

ALLOW 1 hour 45 minutes

START Ponte Tre Archi over the Cannaregio Canal

FINISH Santa Lucia railway station

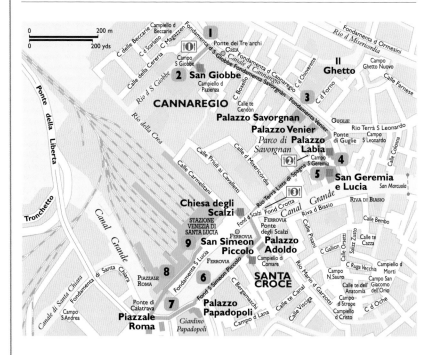

depicted the life of Cleopatra. Tiepolo himself appears in the work as does Elena, the wife of nobleman Nicolò Balbi. She is immortalized as Cleopatra. A story circulated that gives an insight into the Labia family and how they perceived themselves in Venetian society. During a banquet given by the Labias for 40 noblemen, the table was laid with the finest gold cutlery. At the end of the meal the head of the family rose from his chair, collected the gold and threw it out of the window, declaring that with or without

such finery the Labia would always be the Labia. Unknown to everyone, however, a fishing net had been lowered into the canal in a bid to capture the precious articles. Perhaps they were not as rich as they appeared or perhaps just too mean.

4 From Palazzo Labia keep left into Campo San Geremia for the entrance to Chiesa San Geremia e Lucia.

The church of San Geremia e Lucia dates from 1773 and contains the relics of the

virgin martyr, Santa Lucia of Siracusa in Sicily. They were moved here following the demolition of the Convent of Santa Lucia, which made way for the railway station in 1860, as did the neighbouring Monastery of Corpus Domini.

5 Leave Campo San Geremia on the opposite side from the Ponte di Guglie along Rio Terrà Lista di Spagna (at one time a place of diplomatic immunity) to reach Fondamenta degli Scalzi and the Ponte degli Scalzi. Cross the Ponte degli Scalzi and turn right into Fondamenta San Simeon Piccolo. Palazzo Adoldo and the church of San Simeon Piccolo are either side of the entrance to Campiello di Comare.

The church of San Simeon Piccolo was built in the 18th century. Its full name

is the church of Santi Simeone e Guida, after the two disciples Simon and Judas. *Piccolo* means 'small' and is the nickname given to the church to differentiate it from the nearby church of San Simeon Profeta or San Simeon Grande. The *grande* or 'large' church is paradoxically three times smaller than the *piccolo*, as the original church of Santi Simeone e Guida, dating from the 10th century, was much smaller. The church of San Simeon Piccolo is the only church in Venice where mass is celebrated in Latin.

6 Continue along Fondamenta San Simeon Piccolo, crossing over Rio dei Tolentini to reach the Giardino Papadopoli.

Palazzo Papadopoli has an elegant façade on the Grand Canal but you may prefer to rest tired feet in the Papadopoli Gardens. To enter the park take a left turn into Fondamenta Monastero and follow it as it bears right.

7 Keep close to the Grand Canal and cross over another small bridge to Piazzale Roma at the foot of the new bridge over the canal, designed by Spaniard Santiago Calatrava.

The 2008 Calatrava bridge is the fourth bridge to span the Grand Canal and links the only part of Venice where cars are allowed to enter the city. From the bridge it is possible to get a good view of the Grand Canal as it begins its path towards Piazza San Marco. The bridge connects this district to the train station

although the bridge is strictly pedestrian. This area is of particular historical and religious interest. In 1262 the Monastery of Santa Chiara (now the site of a hotel) was left a gift of a small box by a pilgrim returning from the Holy Land. The box seemed to have special powers. As well as light occasionally emanating from inside the box, the winter flood waters would always stop before reaching it. Eventually, the box was opened; inside there was a nail and a parchment, describing how the former had fastened Jesus' feet to the cross. It is said the pilgrim who brought the reliquary to Venice was Saint Louis, King of France, who had previously died in the crusades. The nail remained in the monastery until 1830, when it was transferred to the church of San Pantalon.

8 Having crossed the bridge walk ahead along Fondamenta Santa Lucia to the entrance of the railway station.

The original spirit of Venice was perhaps buried forever when the Austrians built the railway bridge linking Mestre to the lagoon city. The bridge was constructed between 1841 and 1846, and at the time was the longest in the world at over 11,480ft (3,500m), boasting 233 arches and just 984ft (300m) less than the full length of the Grand Canal. Prior to this the only way to reach the mainland without a boat was during the rare cold weather, when the lagoon froze over. Records note the years of 568, 852, 1118, 1122, 1244 and 1432 and 1491 as significantly cold and icy. The last freeze was in 1928, with the most rigid freeze

WHERE TO EAT

🍽 OSTERIA AI CANOTTIERI, Cannaregio 690, Fondamenta di San Giobbe;
Tel: 041 717 999.
The *osteria* takes its name from Venetian oarsman, and the maritime theme is carried on inside. The grey shrimps with white polenta and the seafood spaghetti are recommended. Good wines. €€

🍽 RISTORANTE AL BRINDISI, Cannaregio 307, Campo S. Geremia; Tel: 041 716 968.
Having just celebrated its centenary, the young staff of the Al Brindisi continue to serve up creative twists on Venetian cuisine. €€

🍽 BREK, Cannaregio 124, Rio Terrà Lista di Spagna;
No phone.
Brek may be a chain self-service restaurant but the food is tasty and you can be sure of getting a seat. €

recorded in the winter of 1864, when it was possible to walk to the islands of San Cristoforo and San Michele from Fondamenta Nuove.

9 Santa Lucia railway station is the point from where almost all Venice's visitors enter the city. You can take the vaporetto the full length of the Grand Canal to St Mark's Square.

131

THE CHURCH OF SAN GEREMIA E LUCIA BOASTS A FINE CAMPANILE

A Refuge in the Swamps

This is an easy walk in a district of the city least frequented by visitors. It is also the area that has been most modified over the centuries.

It was clear from the start that Venice would have to forge its own future. Following the fall of the Roman Empire and the arrival of the Germanic tribes from the north, the islands off the mainland offered the perfect refuge for the citizens of Aquileia and other Roman coastal towns. The shifting sand banks and channels of the lagoon guaranteed protection, and the founding fathers of the new Marine Republic created a meritocratic society. The activities of merchants, bankers, artisans and entrepreneurs were actively encouraged and supported, while a rotation of the Doge and his elected advisors kept any single family or business grouping from holding too much power. The Republic promoted foreign trade by matching any intended investment by private enterprise in return for pouring eventual profits back into the city infrastructure. It was also used to promote the common good, in areas such as law and order, and progressive diplomacy. This policy allowed Venice to grow fast and by 1500 the inhabitants numbered over 120,000, the third largest conurbation in Europe.

1 From the Grand Canal walk straight down Fondamenta dei Tolentini, keeping left to the entrance of the church of San Nicolò da Tolentino.

The church of San Nicolò da Tolentino was inaugurated in 1602 by Doge Marino Grimani in recognition of the Theatines who fled to Venice from Rome following the sack of the Eternal City in 1527. San Nicolò was their church, designed by Palladio, and shows all his distinctive classical hallmarks. You can see eight Corinthian columns at the entrance. The Theatines remained in Venice for another 200 years until they fled again, this time from Napoleon.

2 Exit the church of San Nicolò da Tolentino into Campo dei Tolentini and continue along Fondamenta Tolentini and turn left into Fondamenta Minotto.

The Monastery of the Theatines, adjacent to the church of San Nicolò da Tolentino is now a faculty of architecture at Venice University. The entrance was designed by former lecturer Carlo Scarpa and is as modern as architecture gets in Venice, even though its 1960s design now looks a little dated. Another architectural detail in this area is the concentration of typical Venetian chimneys seen on the opposite side of the canal.

3 Continue along Fondamenta Minotto to the Rio di Malconton bridge on the right. Cross over the bridge keeping left alongside the Rio di Malcanton canal.

Malcanton means 'trouble' and the canal was infamous for people ending up in the water, voluntarily or otherwise. It was also where old scores were settled, especially between the two factions of Venice, the Castellani and Nicolotti families, famous for their institutionalized battles on the Ponte dei Pugni. Today, it could not be more tranquil.

4 Continue along the Rio di Malcanton canal passing a curious tree growing out of the ground floor window of a building. Keep ahead and take a right into Fondamenta del Rio Novo. Carry on until you reach the Ponte del Pagan.

Ponte del Pagan is in fact made up of three bridges that form a single canal crossing. Even having crossed dozens of

135

DISTANCE 2 miles (3.2km)

ALLOW 1 hour 45 minutes

START Grand Canal near Palazzo Papadopoli and Gardens

FINISH Papadopoli Gardens

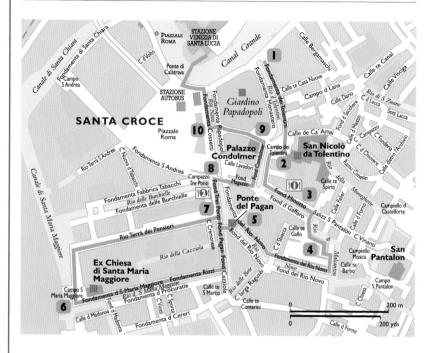

bridges during a visit to Venice, there is something special about this one. From the top of Ponte del Pagan eight further bridges can be viewed simultaneously. It looks and feels like you are in Amsterdam.

5 Cross over the Ponte del Pagan, turn right, then left, into Fondamenta Pagan which becomes Fondamenta Cazzola. Turn right into Fondamenta Rizzi just before the next set of bridges. From here carry on to the former Chiesa di Santa Maria Maggiore.

The monks of the church of Sant Agnese Caterina obtained permission from the Senate to build a church and monastery on this spot. The former church of Santa Maria Maggiore now forms part of a small prison complex, but at one time the area was populated by cloth dyers. The Serenissima regulated the trade by specifying the times of year for undertaking the dying process. This was especially the case for those colours linked tightly with the Republic power and ceremony, such as scarlet. The secrets

of the trade were vigorously guarded, especially at the time of the preparation of the dyes. So much so that the workers invented stories of ghosts and phantoms to keep people away. Tales of assassins in black cloaks carrying lanterns would circulate and apprentices were dressed up to give credence to the stories. These costumes duly entered into the traditions of carnival.

6 From the former Chiesa di Santa Maria Maggiore turn right into **Campo Santa Maria Maggiore and right again into Rio Terrà dei Pensieri.**

Rio Terrà dei Pensieri was so called as it was widely regarded as an ideal location for meditation. The vicinity of the prison that blocked the light also rendered the nearby canals deep and black, a tempting escape from life's problems. The church of Santa Maria Maggiore was built in 1497 after a hermit saw a vision of a woman and child walking on the surface of water, later confirmed by local fishermen.

ABOVE: THE ENGLISH-INSPIRED GIARDINO PAPADOPOLI ARE A GOOD SPOT FOR A REST

7 At the end of Rio Terrà dei Pensieri you rejoin Fondamenta Pagan. Turn left and walk ahead to Campazzo dei Tre Ponti.

Near Campazzo dei Tre Ponti are numerous *burchielli*. The *burchielli* were wooden boats especially popular with Venetian nobles with villas along the Brenta Riviera. They were used to ferry guests and family leisurely, and in luxury, to and from Venice. Today, the main company operating such cruises along this waterway has borrowed the name. Such vessels were constructed in Fondamenta delle Burchielle. The nearby Trattoria alle Burchiello dates from 1503 and has been serving Venetians ever since.

8 Leave Campazzo dei Tre Ponti by crossing the bridge into Fondamenta Magazèn. Carry on ahead and then take a left turn into Fondamenta Condulmer.

On the left along Fondamanta Condulmer is the small Calle dei Lavadori de Lana or 'street of the wool workers'. Wool was an important trading item in the 14th century and provided a solid income for the Republic. It was imported from the Maghreb or North Africa, with the more prized raw material coming from Spain and England. The wool was then exported again to the industrial clothing centres of the River Po plain and Tuscany.

9 Pass Palazzo Condulmer and turn left into the entrance for the Papadopoli Gardens.

WHERE TO EAT

🍴 **TRATTORIA LA ROSADIER VENTI,**
Santa Croce 164, Fondamenta Minotto;
Tel: 041 244 0083.
Only opened in 2008, this pleasant trattoria serves typical Venetian cuisine in a spacious dining room overlooking the canal. €€

🍴 **TRATTORIA AL BURCHIELLO,**
Castello 5854, Fondamenta delle Burchielle;
Tel: 041 522 8989.
The trattoria dates from 1503 and is named after the traditional boats that were made in the area. €€

The Papadopoli Gardens or Giardino Papadopoli are slightly disappointing. They do form a green barrier between Santa Croce and the concrete bunker that is Piazzale Roma, but the spot must have looked much more attractive in the 16th century, when it was a botanical garden attached to Palazzo Papadopoli.

10 Exit the gardens by the way you came in and turn right to Fondamaneta Papadopoli, crossing over the Rio Novo canal and Piazzale Roma. Walking towards the Grand Canal take the newly-built Calatrava footbridge to get to the area close to the railway station. Here you can pick up a vaporetto to a destination of your choice.

Eight Hundred Years of Luxury

This long walk explores Venice's best stores and shopping areas, from designer outlets to the smallest family-run boutiques.

Murano glass and Burano lace are the most prominent of Venice's artisan traditions to have survived to the present day, but at its height the Republic produced a diverse range of handmade items, which were eagerly sought after. Ceremonial coats made from stoat fur, elegant earrings and fans, ornate hats and wigs, jewel-encrusted ladies' shoes, silk socks and stockings were all made in Venice. Occasions such as the Doge's election and annual festivals were ideal events to showcase the Republic's wares and invite buyers from all over Europe. Today, many young artisans still try to preserve and progress this tradition of quality artisan products, and their workshops can be found in all corners of the city. Ironically for Venice (the home of Marco Polo), the invasion of cheap goods from China brings stiff competition, particularly in the case of carnival masks. The most authentic versions are made by hand, using papier mâché, and all are hand-painted.

1 From Harry's Bar on Fondamenta di Farine by the San Marco Vallaresso vaporetto stop, turn right into Calle Vallaresso. Go ahead to Salizzada S. Moisè and turn left. Continue along Salizzada S. Moisè until you reach Campo San Moisè.

Located along Calle Vallaresso, the Ridotto Grande was Venice's first gaming house, dating from 1638. The Serenissima had tried to control illegal gambling for over four centuries. Rules were introduced to ban gambling from the atrium of the Basilica of St Mark's in 1254, and then the ban was extended to the Palazzo Ducale and other areas close to the centre. Only chess was allowed by the turn of the century. But such was the Ventians' passion for gambling that the authorities were fighting a losing battle, and at the beginning of the 17th century the ban was lifted for the whole period of Carnival, which at the time lasted almost five months from October. With the opening of the Ridotto (the world's first pubically-run casino), a new era of gambling and frivolity was ushered in.

2 Leave Campo San Moisè by crossing over the Ponte San Moisè into Calle Larga XXII Marzo. This wide street becomes Calle Bergamaschi and ends with a sharp left turn along Calle de le Ostreghe, over the Ponte de le Ostreghe into Campo Santa Maria del Giglio.

Calle Larga XXII Marzo came into existence just over 100 years ago when Calle San Moisè was widened. Moisè

WHERE TO EAT

🍴 LA CARAVELLA,
San Marco 2398, Via XXII Marzo,
Calle dietro la Chiesa;
Tel: 041 520 8901.
An extremely elegant restaurant located inside the Hotel Saturnia International. Traditional and creative Venetian cuisine is presented with impeccable service. €€€

🍴 HOSTARIA AI CORISTI,
San Marco 1995, Teatro La Fenice;
Tel: 041 522 6677.
Just a few yards from La Fenice theatre, this is the perfect spot for a quiet and relaxed candlelit dinner, before or after the performance. €€

🍴 CENTRALE RESTAURANT LOUNGE,
Piscina Frezzeria 1659;
Tel: 041 296 0664.
Trendy upmarket restaurant with an intimate candlelit interior, with lounge bar and chill-out music. This is possibly the most stylish place in Venice. €€

is a reference to Mosè Venier who built the church of San Moisè in the 10th century. Practically the entire history of the Republic separates the two building projects. Calle Larga XXII Marzo is the street where Italy's most prestigious fashion brands – from clothes to jewellery and shoes – as well as international names can be found.

141

DISTANCE **2.5 miles (4km)**

ALLOW **2 hours 30 minutes**

START **Harry's Bar opposite San Marco Vallaresso vaporetto stop**

FINISH **Ponte di Rialto (Rialto Bridge)**

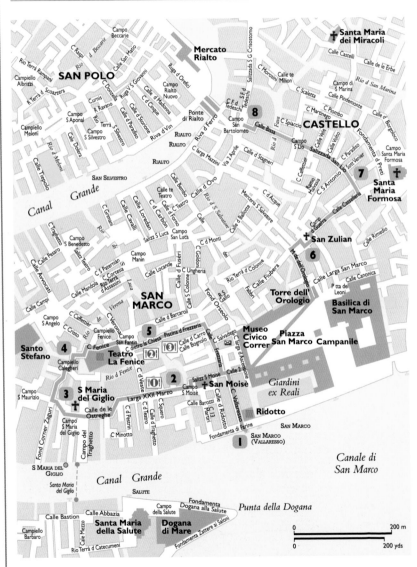

3 Leave Campo Santa Maria del Giglio by crossing the Ponte Duodo o Barbarico bridge and a second bridge, Ponte Paguri. Turn immediately right into Fondamenta de la Malvasia Vecchia and then over the de la Malvasia Vecchia bridge. Cut through Campiello Calegheri and follow Rio Terrà Calagheri.

The back entrance of the La Fenice theatre is particularly evocative, and contrasts with its imposing front. This entrance was clearly designed for water access only, and it is easy to imagine the gondolas lining up to unload passengers before and after a performance. The name *calegheri* refers to the cobblers or shoemakers who set up stalls here.

4 Leave Rio Terrà Calagheri by turning right over the Rio Menu o de le Verona. Proceed right along the exterior of the Teatro la Fenice, along Calle Fenice, until you come to Campo San Fantin. Leave Campo San Fantin by Calle dietro la Chiesa.

Many of Venice's street names refer to the city's old trades, which were each concentrated in a particular location. In this most upmarket of Venice's shopping districts is Calle Frezzeria. The name is local dialect for *frecce* or 'arrow'. Nearby is Sotoportego and Corte della Polvere, a clear reference to powder – not gunpowder, but cosmetic powder – produced here by a local family in 1763. The powder was used to whiten the wigs worn by both men and women in the 18th century. Sold in perfume shops, it was the precursor to our present-day face powder.

5 Cross over the Ponte dei Piscina into Piscina di Frezzeria. Go ahead to Calle Frezzeria and turn right. Continue along Calle Frezzeria to Salizzada San Moisè. Taking the left turn leads into Calle Seconda de l'Ascension and St Mark's Square. Cross the square and pass under Torre dell'Orologio into Merceria dell'Orologio. Continue until Campo S. Zulian opens on the right.

Campo San Zulian was the first area to suffer damage at the hands of the populace after they realized the Serenissima was about to abdicate power to Napoleon. Their fury was first vented on the Zorzi pharmacy (drugstore), situated near the Campo. This was then followed by an attack on the private houses of two eminent lawyers. A San Stae cheese store was raided, as was a local bookshop, believed to be full of French propaganda material, and a tailor's workshop that had supplied uniforms for the French army. Worst of all was the sacking of the magnificent Palazzo dei Foscarini ai Carmini, used to house royal visitors, which was devastated. Valuable paintings were slashed, windows smashed and beautiful furniture thrown from the windows. Even the terrace mosaics were stamped into pieces.

6 Leave Campo S. Zulian by edging around the right of the church into Calle dei Segretari, then left into Calle S. Zulian and right at Campo della Guerra to cross the Ponte della Guerra. Take an immediate right and follow Calle Casselleria to turn left again into Salizzada S. Lio.

Located in Salizzada S. Lio at Corte Perina was the house of Giovanni Antonio Canal, better known as artist Canaletto (1697–1768). As a painter of views of Venice, Canaletto could not be better named. Having adopted the *veduta* (view) technique his fame swiftly spred to Europe, especially to England, where he was asked to stay and paint scenes of London. At first, the English authorities thought they had commissioned the wrong man, as his paintings of London did not match up to those of Venice. Art critic John Ruskin (1819–1900) was one of those who slated his works. But Canaletto had simply developed his style. Interestingly, he always painted from memory and his best work should be viewed from the mid-distance. As you get closer the composition seems to go out of focus.

7 Salizzada S. Lio leads into Campo S. Lio and Calle Ponte S. Antonio. Cross over the bridge and along Sotoportego del Sgaleter to continue under Sotoportego de la Bissa to conclude the walk in Campo San Bartolomeo.

The pharmacy Alla Testa d'Oro was once located between Campo San Bartolomeo and the Rialto bridge. Although the shop no longer sells prescription drugs, the old sign can be clearly seen above the No. 3318. As well as Greek and Arab influence, links with the Far East meant that many herbs and spices found their way into the Republic. The Venetians became masters of preparing herbal remedies, mixed together in huge mortars with large pestles. One such recipe was called *theriaca*, by all accounts a powerful potion to banish any ailment. Look again above the sign to vaguely make out the original name of the shop 'Theriaca Andromachi'.

8 Campo San Bartolomeo stands at the foot of the Rialto Bridge. Cross over to find a restaurant by the canal.

145

THE BROAD SWEEP OF THE GRAND CANAL VIEWED FROM THE PONTE DEGLI SCALZI

Artisans of Venice

This short walk passes many small, fascinating artisan shops and Venetian workshops, their owners determined to keep the traditional crafts alive.

By the 13th century and before the discovery of new trade routes around the Cape of Good Hope and to the New World, Venice dominated commerce across the Mediterranean. Skills imported and refined on the lagoon islands helped to create the first 'Made in Italy' industry. The exquisite Murano glass is well documented, but the Republic's expertise extended to the manufactur of such items as rare furs, gold-encrusted leather goods and silk cloth. Even the production of mirrors boomed, so much so that the Corporation of Mirror Workers doubled its members in the 16th century. To further appreciat the industrious spirit of the period, visit the textile section of the museum of S Mark's Basilica. Here are displayed some of the oldest of all European tapestries and other products, indicating the extent of commercial trade throughout the Republic's history. There are 12th-century Byzantine pieces, carpets from 17th-century Isphahan donated by the Shah of Persia and many other trophies

From Museo Casa Carlo Goldoni turn right along Calle dei Nomboli, then take the first left into Rio Terrà dei Nomboli and first right into Calle dei Saoneri. Go ahead and cross over the Ponte San Polo into Salizzada San Polo, and walk on into Campo San Polo.

Campo San Polo took its present form in 1750 when the Sant'Antonio canal was filled in. It immediately became popular as a venue for masked balls during Carnival and even hosted races and bullfights. It is the focal point for the *sestiere* (district) of San Polo, which tends to merge seamlessly with Santa Croce. Polo is derived from Paulo or Paul, a reference to the saint to whom the 12th-century church in the campo is dedicated. Inside are 14 magnificent paintings by Tiepolo of the *Via Crucis*.

ASSOCIAZIONE CHIESE DI VENEZIA;

www.chorusvenezia.org

2 Leave Campo San Polo by Calle della Madonnetta and pass over the Ponte della Madonnetta.

Just to the right before the bridge are the offices of the Biennale. The actual archives of the Biennale or Archivio Storico d'Arte Contemporanea della Biennale are housed in Palazzo Corner della Regina along the Grand Canal. Translated into English this is 'The Corner Palace of the Queen', and the queen in question is Caterina Corner. Already born into the Venetian aristocracy in this very palace in 1454, Caterina eventually married into the royal family of Cyprus. To keep her politically onside

WHERE TO EAT

[O] OSTERIA AL PONTE 'LA PATATINA',
San Polo 2741/A, Calle Saoneri;
Tel: 041 523 7238.
Lively tavern offering a quick lunch of typical Venetian cuisine. €€

[O] OSTERIA VIVALDI,
San Polo 1457, near Campiello Meloni;
Tel: 041 523 8185.
A traditional osteria in which to try a typical meal of swordfish carpaccio, potato gnocchi with prawns and courgettes with a tomato and mozzarella salad. €€

[O] BIRRERIA ANTICA CORTE,
Campo San Polo 2168;
Tel: 041 275 0570.
Relaxed, stylish restaurant and pizzeria in which to enjoy the early evening in the company of friends. The Antica Corte was formerly a brewery. €

she was given a pension of 8,000 gold *ducati* and a feudal home in the beautiful Veneto town of Asolo. As you cross the bridge notice to your right a shop selling silk items, including a line of beautiful fur-lined silk hats that give the impression of being brought here from the court of Kubla Khan, at the time of Marco Polo.

3 At the end of Calle della Madonnetta turn left into Calle del Luganegher. Keep left into Calle dei Cavalli and cross

DISTANCE 1.5 miles (2.4km)

ALLOW 1 hour 30 minutes

START Museo Casa Carlo Goldoni

FINISH Ponte degli Scalzi

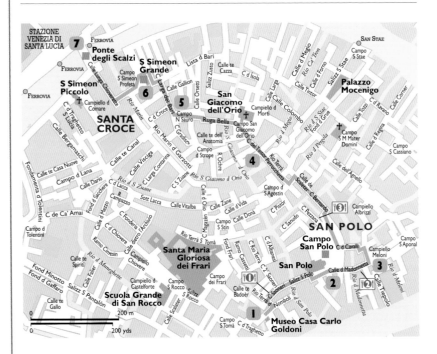

over bridge back into Campo San Polo. Keep right and exit the square through Rio Terrà S. Antonio, which turns right into Calle Bernardo. Cross over the Ponte San Bernardo and continue along Calle Scaletér to turn left into Rio Terrà Secondo, then right into Rio Terrà Parrucchetta.

The name of this street refers to the strange wig (*parrucha*) worn by one of the commercial traders who worked here. He was a source of ridicule and fun.

4 Crossing over the Ponte del Parrucchetta continue along Calle del Tintor and Campo San Giacomo dell'Orio. Keep to the left and take the second bridge on the left, Ponte Ruga Bella o del Forner. Ruga Bella continues into Campo N. Sauro.

Campo Sauro is named after Nazario N. Sauro, a martyr from World War I, when Italy lost its colonies in Istria and Dalmatia. There was effectively a genocide of Italian nationals and Sauro's

remains rest in Palazzo Farsetti along the Grand Canal, symbolizing his eventual glorious return to his homeland.

5 Exit Campo N. Sauro by Calle Larga dei Bari in the top right corner. Go ahead until the left turn into Salizzada della Chiesa. A left turn follows the church walls into Campo San Simeon Profeta and the church entrance.

The church of San Simeon Grande or San Simeon Profeta is actually smaller than its sister, San Simeon Piccolo. The latter is three times the size and is one of the first of Venice's impressive landmarks to catch the eye of anyone arriving from Santa Lucia train station. It was originally the city's largest and more important religious building. Inside Simeon Grande are the relics of St Simeon, brought to Venice in 1205, and to whom the building is dedicated.

6 Leaving the church, cross Campo San Simeon Profeta. Cross over a small bridge and turn right into Calle Lunga Chioverette to the foot of the Ponte degli Scalzi.

Ponte degli Scalzi is surprisingly recent, dating from the mid-19th century and reconstructed in 1932. It is made entirely of stone from Istria, replacing the original built by the Austrians. The Roman baroque church, close to the bridge, is the Chiesa di Santa Maria di Nazareth o dei Carmelitani Scalzi, to give it its full name. The religious order here was originally from Rome and *scalzi* in Italian

means 'barefoot.' The church was built only a few years before the Great Fire of London of 1666 by Baldassarre Longhena, the same man who was responsible for the iconic Santa Maria della Salute church, and it is the only religious building in the city with an exterior

of marble, from Carrara in Tuscany. Longhena may have been shocked to see London go up in flames, but he could never have imagined the damage done to the church when an Austrian bomb fell through the roof in 1915. A vault frescoed by Tiepolo was destroyed, with just a few fragments in the Gallerie dell'Accademia reminding us of what has been lost.

7 Finish by crossing the Ponte degli Scalzi and taking a vaporetto along the Grand Canal to a convenient point near to your hotel.

153

Fish Tales and Fish Tails

This fairly easy walk through the busy Venetian streets ends on the northern shores at the church of San Francesco della Vigna.

'*Venezia è un Pesce*' or '*Venice is a Fish*' according to author Tiziano Scarpa in his book of the same name about the city. In fact, if you look at a modern map of the city, the shape of the lagoon city looks rather like a goldfish or fat herring. Recently, this analogy has been taken further and the fish shape has become a new logo for the city. This walk takes you from south to north, roughly cutting off the tail of the fish. It begins quite near to Piazza San Marco, which is the lowest point of the city at just 25in (64cm) above sea level, measured exactly at the central door of the Basilica of San Marco. It ends by the relatively deep swell and in full blast of the northern winds off the Fondamenta Nuove. The Fondamenta was constructed as part of a major town-planning scheme in the 16th century, which established the northern limits of Venice. The area is full of small streets that reflect the life and trades of those who lived here then, such as coopers or rope makers.

1 From Campo San Filippo e Giacomo bear right and exit the Campo by Calle della Chiesa. Before the bridge, turn left into Campo S. Giovanni in Oleo and the church of S. Giovanni Novo in Oleo. Keeping right, enter Fondamenta di Rimedio under the covered walkway.

Campo San Filippo e Giacomo is an extremely lively market square close to St Mark's Square, in direct contrast to the stillness and tranquillity of Campo S. Giovanni in Oleo. Heading past Palazzo Soranzo, the canals and corners are especially picturesque, so much so that Russian composer Piotr Ilyich Tchaikovsky (1840–93) was inspired to compose his fourth symphony in a nearby hotel in December 1877.

2 Leave this area and cross right over the bridge and into Campo Santa Maria Formosa.

The church of Santa Maria Formosa is in the form of a Greek Cross. On 2 February every year the Doge of Venice would pay his respects, offering a symbolic toll at the entrance. During the ceremony he would receive two straw hats, a basket of oranges and two flagons of wine. The event followed a promise made by Doge Pietro Candiano to remember the heroic actions of the casket makers, who on the 31 January 944 saved the 12 virgins, who traditionally opened and closed Carnival from the hands of Istrian pirates.

ASSOCIAZIONE CHIESE DI VENEZIA;

www.chorusvenezia.org

3 Exit Campo Santa Maria Formosa by Campiello S. Maria Formosa and follow Calle Lunga S. Maria Formosa until two bridges come into view. Do not take the first, but keep left and take the second, Ponte Tetta, into the very narrow Calle Tetta. This exits onto another bridge, Ponte del'Ospedaletto. Continue along Calle Ospedale to Barbaria delle Tole.

The Venetian nobles kept their horses in the Cavallerizza near Barbaria delle Tole. The name has clear equestrian connotations, as it was here they practiced their skills, until the riding of horses and presence of horse carriages was banned by the Republic to protect the frail

DISTANCE 1.5 miles (2.4km)

ALLOW 1 hour 45 minutes

START Campo San Filippo e Giacomo near Piazza San Marco

FINISH Fondamenta Nuove vaporetto stop

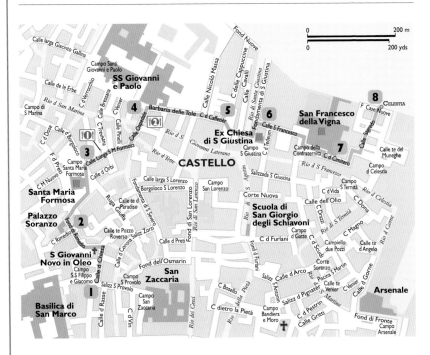

wooden bridges from collapsing. The first ban dates from around 1287, when merchants were obliged to tie up their mounts at the Mercerie before entering San Marco on foot. A similar law applied to the Rialto district. Being primarily people with an affiliation with water, the Venetians were not considered the best horsemen and were often derided by visitors from the mainland. Horses went on to become status symbols and were often decorated and painted, using a plant from Cyprus to colour them orange.

4 Turn right and then follow straight along Barbaria delle Tole until you reach Calle del Caffetièr.

The Barbaria delle Tole was an area of warehouses and workshops used to store and saw wood for making tables. 'Barbaria' may refer to the market for the end products, a reference to North Africa, or possibly the mountain men who undertook the hard work. Also manufactured in this area were the artificial beauty spots worn by fashionable

women. In Italian they are known as *mosche* or *moschete*, which also doubles as a word for less attractive flies. They were made in various shapes to symbolize moods, and where on the face they were worn was also significant. For example, if placed at the corner of the eye, it communicated passion.

5 Go ahead into Campo de Giustina detto de Barbaria and leave the square by Calle Zen, which opens onto the Ponte Fondamenta S. Giustina.

The former church of Santa Giustina was rebuilt between 1636 and 1640 to commemorate the victory over the Turks at the Battle of Lepanto in 1571. It was for a time used as a secondary school.

6 Turn left along the Fondamenta to turn first right into Calle San Francesco, which leads to Campo San Francesco Vigna.

When the relics of St Mark were brought to Venice from Jerusalem in 828, it was

ABOVE: ST MARK IS REVERED IN THE SAN FRANCESCO DELLA VIGNA CHURCH

not the first time the Patron Saint visited the city. On his way from Aquileia he had been shipwrecked in the lagoon during a storm and had to seek refuge near the present day church of San Francesco della Vigna. In his sleep an angel told him he would return and this would be where his body would be laid to rest. This vision gave the Serenissima its motto '*Pax tibi Marce Evangelista Meum*' (Peace to you, Mark my Evangelist). Vigna refers to the many vines that once grew here on grounds belonging to Marco Ziani, the count of Arbe and son of Doge Pietro. On his death, he donated the plot to Franciscan monks, who built a small church dedicated to St Mark. The monks remain, and in 1989 founded the Institute of Ecumenical Studies that contains an important collection of antique and modern religious books.

7 Leave the church from Campo della Confraternita and bear left into Calle Dietro la Chiesa, which becomes Calle d. Cimitero. Turn left again into Calle Sagredo, which leads to Fondamenta Case Nuove.

A rather lonely arch sits just before reclaimed land in Fondamenta Case Nuove where a group of new houses has been built. This area borders the Arsenale and the northern shore from which Venetian galleys set sail. Originally crewed by paid citizens, by the mid-16th century the Republic decided to use convicts as slave labour, and a distinction was made between free men working on the ships and those in the galleys, rowing

WHERE TO EAT

[O] TRATTORIA AL MASCARON,
Castello 5225, Calle Lunga Santa Maria Formosa;
Tel: 041 522 5995.
Evokes the traditional atmosphere of an old *osteria*, with wooden fittings and many mementoes on the walls. The cuisine is strictly Veneto. €€

[O] OSTERIA ALLA STAFFA,
Castello 6397, Calle dell'Ospedaletto;
Tel: 041 523 9160.
Warm, local bar not often frequented by tourists, and serving classic snacks such as salami from Friuli Venezia Giulia to *cicchetti* (little snacks like tapas) and local wines. €

in 'gaol' formation, unable to move from their position in the boat. Such were the ties between the crews, state and officials that the anchorage of the ships was rented from private individuals who saw it as way of serving the Republic. A Venetian sea captain was also entitled to keep the coat of arms of his vessel, which were positioned on the stern, when he retired.

HELLO VENEZIA VISITOR INFORMATION;
www.hellovenezia.it

8 Take the vaporetto from the Fondamenta Nuove to the Grand Canal, making sure that the boat is heading towards Santa Lucia railway station and not St Mark's Square.

A TONDO OF ST NICOLAS IN GLORY EMBLAZENS THE CEILING OF SAN NICOLÓ DEI MENDICOLI CHURCH

Rising Tides and Watermarks

High tides in Venice occur from November to February. This walk gives you a real sense of the city's close relationship with the open sea.

There have been two great floods in the history of Venice, both of which seriously risked submerging the city for good. The first was on 15 February 1340, and the second in 1966, when the water level was almost 6.5ft (2m) above average. The latter led to the instigation of many of the territory's current water projects, including the immense Mose project, which will add moving barriers near Malamocco, Lido and Chioggia, where the lagoon opens out into the Adriatic Sea. High-water levels have been recorded throughout the history of the city and the first attempts to stop the tides included the construction of the *murazzia*, a huge dam complex between Malamocco and Chioggia. The aim was also to protect the fragile ecosystem of the lagoon using huge blocks of Istrian stone. The walk begins at the Zattere, which is the long panoramic quay facing Giudecca and named after the boats that transported wood from the forests of the Cadore. With no natural solid foundations, Venice is actually built on the trunks of millions of such trees, which were, and still are, sunk into the lagoon mud, thus preserving the wood from rotting.

I Leave the Ponte Lungo bridge and proceed along Fondamenta Zattere Ponte Lungo.

Across the water, the imposing Mulino Stucky was built as a flour mill in 1883 by Swiss entrepreneur Johan Stucky. This was once the location of the Monastery of St Biagio and Cataldo, dating from 1222. The building of the monastery was requested by Beata Giuliana dei Conti di Collalto, who was noted for her many miracles. On her death, Giuliana was buried in the common cemetery. Twenty five years later, lights started to appear at night in the district, described as stars by historian Flaminio Corner. Although St Giuliana now rests in the church of St Agnese, lights still used to flicker in the abandoned mill, now a luxury hotel.

2 At the San Basilio vaporetto stop turn right into Calle del Vento and on to Campo de San Basegio. Keep right along Fondamenta San Basilio and cross over the Ponte San Sebastian to the church of S. Sebastiano on the other side of the Rio di San Sebastiano.

One of Venice's greatest names, artist Paolo Veronese (1528–88), was laid to rest in the church of San Sebastiano, at the foot of the church organ (indicated by a stone). The church is somewhat overlooked today and seems a humble spot for the artist's final resting place in comparison with his contemporaries, but Veronese was passionate about this building and in his lifetime dedicated many works and frescoes to the church.

Three miles (5km) offshore from the church of San Nicolò are the ruins of the bell tower that collapsed in St Mark's Square in 1902 and was dumped in 46ft (14m) of water. The clearance took six months, and even during stormy tides, fragments from the tower still wash up along the Riva.

ASSOCIAZIONE CHIESE DI VENEZIA;

www.chorusvenezia.org

3 Pass the church to the right into Campo dietro il Cimetero, which flanks Campo Angelo Raffaele. The church of Angelo Raffaele stands here.

According to tradition, the church of Angelo Raffaele was founded in the 7th century by San Magno of

163

DISTANCE 2 miles (3.2km)

ALLOW 2 hours

START Ponte Lungo near the Zattere vaporetto stop

FINISH Scuola Grande dei Carmini

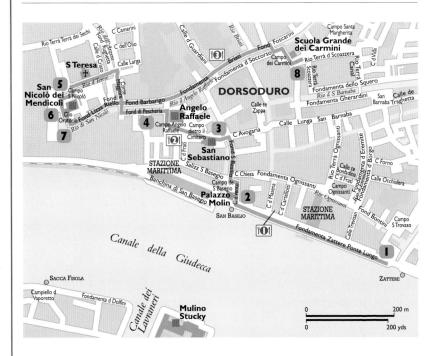

Oderzo, although the present building is a thousand years newer. Most of what we see today dates from the mid-18th century, including scenes from the *Book of Tobias* depicting the Angel Raphael. Look out for two paintings dating from 1588. The first is entitled *The Centurion Before Christ*, the second *Punishment of the Snakes*.

4 Exit the church and turn left along Fondamenta di Pescheria. Continue along the Fondamenta and cross the bridge on the right into Corte Maggiore,

which in Venetian dialect becomes Corte Mazor on the street signs. Go straight ahead and take the first bridge on the left over Rio dell'Arzero to continue along Fondamenta delle Terese (Fondamenta de le Terse in local dialect).

The church of Santa Teresa stands in a district known as Santa Marta, an old working class area from which ferries used to connect Venice to the mainland at Fusina. *Arzene* refers to the embankments in the area caused by a build-up of mud

WHERE TO EAT

⟦O⟧ RISTORANTE LA RIVIERA,
Dorsoduro 1473, Fondamenta
Zattere al Ponte Lungo;
Tel: 041 522 7621.
Elegant and informal restaurant with
a canalside terrace from which to
watch the cruise liners sliding by.
The dishes are seasonal, combining
tradition and innovation. €€

⟦O⟧ PANE VINO E SAN DANIELE,
Dorsoduro 1722, Campo Angelo
Raffaele;
Tel: 041 523 7456.
A young and lively tavern not yet on
the tourist trail and with clear roots
in the cuisine and hospitality of the
Friuli Venezia Giulia region. €

⟦O⟧ OSTERIA DA CODROMA,
Dorsoduro 2540, Fondamenta Briati;
Tel: 041 524 6789.
Traditional snacks, sandwiches and
wines to keep you going during
the day. €

Dating from the 7th century, the church of San Nicolò dei Mendicoli was built on one of the first islands inhabited by Venetians. Parts of the church are ancient and it was founded by the *patavini*, or inhabitants of Padua. The name *mendicoli* may translate as 'poor' or 'residents of the island of Mendigola'. It has been rebuilt a number of times to the original basilica plan, and was fortified at the end of the 14th century when the Genovese fleet threatened to attack the city during the War of Chioggia. What we see today dates from the 16th century. Look out for the typical porch in front of the church from which the poor alms were requested and prayers said for penitents. Near the entrance, a plaque in English reads 'During the years from 1971 to 1977 with the collaboration of the Italian State this church with its precious works of art was saved from the waters and restored to its ancient glory by the British Venice in Peril fund.'

THE BRITISH COMMITTEE FOR THE PRESERVATION OF VENICE;

www.veniceinperil.org

6 Circle around the church to the right to view the marvellous bell tower.

The 12th-century bell tower has been an important beacon and symbol of Venice for centuries. Today, however, it is dominated by industrial buildings built at the time of the new railway. The huge Cotonificio Veneziano is an old cotton mill, dating from 1883 and now home to the architecture faculty of the University of Venice.

deposits from the Brenta Riviera before it was diverted to enter the lagoon further south from Venice. On reclaimed land here you will see many popular 20th-century housing schemes. Look out for the distinctive Case Tron with its seven chimneys.

5 Beyond the church of Santa Teresa cross over the Ponte de San Nicolò into Campo San Nicolò.

7 Walk past the bell tower to Campiello Oratorio and Fondamenta Lizza. Continue along Fondamenta Riello, which leads to Fondamenta Barbarigo. Carry on ahead, passing the bridge to Angelo Raffaelle into Fondamenta Briati. Continue past Sotoportego dei Guardiani on the left and onto Fondamenta Foscarini. Turn right over the Ponte Foscarini into Campo dei Carmini.

Fondamenta Briati is named after Giuseppe Briati, who lived for a number of years in Bohemia, the present-day Czech Republic. The country has always had a fine crystal glass-making tradition and Briati returned to Venice with a set of skills and knowledge that enabled him to set up a factory in this street in 1730. The jealousy shown by the more traditional glass-makers of Murano when Briati set up shop in their backyard resulted in him being threatened and physically attacked. Today, the name Briati is visible in a number of streets in Murano, so peace must eventually have been made.

8 As with Walk 12, finish this walk by cutting through Campo Santa Margherita, exiting via Rio Terrà di Scoazzera before taking a right into Rio Terrà Canal and crossing over the Ponte dei Pugni bridge. From Campo San Barnaba, take Calle del Traghetto to the Ca' Rezzonico vaporetto stop.

167

Walking on Water

This walk begins with a gondola ride and continues with an easy stroll along the Strada Nova. It can be done after a visit to the Rialto market.

The gondola trip across the Grand Canal from the Rialto fish market is not a normal gondola ride, but one which has to be done standing up. There are many ways to cross the Grand Canal, including bridges, vaporetto buses and private water taxis, but this is the by far the most enjoyable. There are plenty of stops indicated on the tourist maps, and the services are simple hops from one side of the Grand Canal to the other for less than one euro. The reason for starting this walk in such a way is to appreciate that many of the original canals have disappeared, filled in to allow greater access to the city by pedestrians. The names of these filled-in canals begin with two words 'Rio Terà, with 'Terà' the Venetian dialect for '*terra*' or earth. Confusingly, you will see both spellings on local maps and signs. This walk takes you along the most important Rio Terrà of all, the Strada Nova, which links the railway station to Campo Santi Apostoli, opened on 2 September 1871. The original plans suggest it was meant to accommodate a tram line, although this never materialized.

Take the gondola bus from the stop at the Rialto fish market by Campo della Pescaria. Arriving at Campo S. Sofia go straight ahead, between Palazzo Foscari and Palazzo Sagredo, and then turn left into Strada Nova.

Palazzo Foscari was built by Doge Francesco Foscari, a formidable political figure and rich power broker. He was Doge for 35 years, until the age of 84. His money came from marrying into a wealthy banking family and making an immense fortune in commerce in Rialto. He had similar ambitions for his son, Jacopo, and married him into the wealthy Contarini family. However, Jacopo soon became involved in a corruption and bribery scandal that was compounded when he killed the judge who was investigating him. Not wanting to draw his father's name into the mess, Jacopo refused to name the Doge as being involved, even under torture. He was subsequently condemned to temporary exile in Crete. He could think himself fortunate to escape a worse punishment, but foolishly, in a fit of pique, he decided to seek revenge against the Serenissima by contacting the Republic's worst enemies, Mehemed II and Francesco Sforza, Duke of Milan, and he was subsequently put to death. Six months after Jacopo's death, the Consiglio dei Dieci demanded Foscari's abdication. In these turbulent times it could have been worse.

2 From here, take the first left into Calle Ca' d'Oro.

WHERE TO EAT

🍽 **OSTERIA AL BOMBA,**
Cannaregio 4297/98, Calle Forno;
Tel: 041 520 5175.
'Who only drinks water has a secret to keep' is the philosophy of La Bomba. Both wine drinking and poetry are on the menu. €€

🍽 **RISTORANTE DA POGGI,**
Cannaregio 2103, Rio Terrà della Maddalena;
Tel: 041 721 199.
Venetian and international recipes are given a new twist by the enthusiastic young chefs. €€

Built by Marino Contarini in the 15th century, Palazzo Ca' d'Oro flourished during Venice's golden period under Doge Francesco Foscari. No expense was spared in its construction and the best craftsmen and artists all contributed. *Oro* refers to the gold overlay that decorated parts of the exterior.

3 Backtrack to Strada Nova. Turn left and walk along to Campiello dei Testori.

Although apparently modernized, with its McDonalds and Lush stores, Strada Nova retains many traces of the past. Above a beauty shop on the left-hand side an old sign is still clearly visible. It reads 'Cinema & Teatro Progress.' Near the Ca' d'Oro vaporetto stop there is huge well, now sealed by a bronze top. Wells were

OPPOSITE: CLASSIC VENETIAN GOTHIC WINDOW DESIGN CAN BE SEEN ALONG THE GRAND CANAL

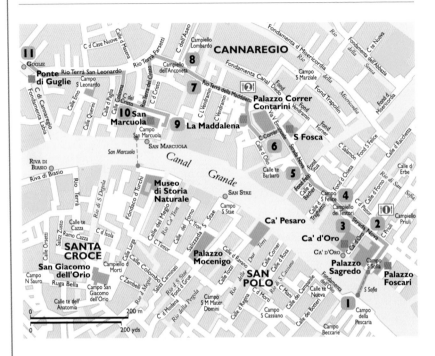

DISTANCE 1.5 miles (2.4km)

ALLOW 1 hour 30 minutes

START Rialto fish market

FINISH Ponte di Guglie over the Cannaregio Canal

both cisterns and filters, providing fresh water for the citizens, and like many trade secrets the art of constructing a good well was passed from father to son. In 1858 a census of wells in Venice revealed over 6,700 wells in the city.

4 Cross over the bridge into Campo San Felice and continue along to Fondamenta Felzi on the left.

Fondmaneta Felzi is named after the artisans who used to make the hooded

cabins for gondolas. The cabins are still made today, and are part of the 12 specialist crafts required to produce a gondola, which include oar-making, sculpting the *forcole* where the oars rest, and even the craft of the milliners and cobblers who manufacture the traditional hats and shoes still worn by gondoliers.

5 Turn left out of Fondamenta Felzi back into Strada Nova by crossing over the bridge. Continue until Strada Nova runs into Via V. Emanuele. Turn left

170

OPPOSITE: VENETIAN LIONS ADORN THE FAÇADE OF THE CA' D'ORO

into Calle Correr, just before you reach Palazzo Correr Contarini.

Before turning into Calle Correr, note the church of Santa Fosca and the little campo of the same name just beyond it. The campo boasts a small fruit and vegetable market in the mornings, while the bronze statue is a monument to Paolo Sarpi, a religious advisor to the Serenissima during the late 16th and early 17th centuries. A thinker, scientist and historian, Sarpi was a dangerous man. He was attacked on the bridge off the square in October 1607 having defended the Republic against the wishes of Pope Paul V. The bridge was called Ponte della Guerra, or 'Bridge of War', and, like Ponte dei Pugni, was a place where ritual fighting regularly took place between different factions of the city. The four white marble footprints indicate the starting positions for these group scuffles.

6 Cross over the Ponte Correr and turn right under Sotoportego de le Colonete that exits by the La Maddalena church in Campo Maddalena. Keep left into Rio Terrà della Maddalena.

Look out for the austere church known as La Maddalena, in particular the symbol above the solid bottle-green door. It is more than likely a masonic reference, ordered by the head of the Balbo family when the church was rebuilt in 1780, just seven years before the Republic fell.

7 Backtrack to Rio Terrà della Maddalena and turn left to cross over the Ponte de l'Anconeta and into Calle dell'Anconeta. Go ahead to Campiello dell'Anconeta.

This is where one of Venice's liveliest markets is held, right in the middle of the Strada Nova. Close by is a wonderful

ABOVE: THE SAN MARCUOLA CHURCH CONTAINS ARTISTIC MASTERPIECES; OPPOSITE: DETAIL ON THE PONTE DI GUGLIE

coffee shop called Antica Torrefazione di Caffè, dating from 1930. Two painted masked characters in carnival costume either side of the door invite the visitor in, and the smell of freshly ground coffee does the rest. The interior is full of bags of coffee beans, just as it was almost 80 years ago.

8 Leave Campiello dell'Anconeta by turning left into Rio Terrà Farsetti, and take the first left into Rio Terrà del Cristo to reach the church of San Marcuola in Campo San Marcuola.

The church in this delightful corner of Venice, between the Strada Nova and the Grand Canal, is dedicated to two saints; Ermagora and Fortunato. According to common belief, it was founded in the 10th century by refugees fleeing the Longobards (Lombards) on the mainland. The church contains a beautiful *Last Supper* by Tintoretto (1518–94) and an altar by Giovanni Morlatier (1699–1781). Morlatier also created the main altar in the Chiesa della Salute and produced sculptures for the Gesuati church.

9 Backtrack around the church to Calle del Cristo.

In Calle del Cristo, there is a stone post set behind the church of San Marcuola. Carved into it is an image of Jesus on the cross with the cross itself sitting on a skull and cross bones. This is a literal reference to the Calvary or Golgotha, the hill where the crucifixion took place. The date on the column is 1668.

10 Continue along Calle del Cristo to Calle Colonna and then turn right, exiting in Rio Terrà S Leonardo and the Ponte di Guglie.

Dating from 1580, the single-span Ponte di Guglie crosses the Canale di Cannaregio. This is where the vaporetto boats enter the Grand Canal from the northern shore and the islands of Murano and Burano. It is an obligatory crossing to reach the Santa Lucia railway station on foot. Guglie is a reference to the four 'spires' found on the balustrades. Look out for the cartoon-like *mascaron* (mask) heads on the arch of the bridge.

11 Having walked on water all this way, take a boat from the Guglie vaporetto stop back to the Grand Canal and further connections.

INDEX

ACKNOWLEDGEMENTS

The Automobile Association wishes to thank the following photographers and picture libraries for their assistance in the preparation of this book. Abbreviations for the picture credits are as follows: (AA) AA World Travel Library

Front Cover Alamy/Topcris; 3 4Corners/SIME/Scattolin Sebastiano; 8 photolibrary.com/De Agostini Editore; 11 AA/Dario Miterdiri; 12 AA/Clive Sawyer; 14 AA/Anna Mockford and Nick Bonetti; 15 Alamy/G Owston (Italy); 17 AA/Clive Sawyer; 18 photolibrary.com/Hemis; 20 4Corners/SIME/Fantuz Olimpio; 22 photolibrary.com/Jon Arnold Travel; 25 Alamy/Worldwide Picture Library; 27 Alamy/Martin Norris; 28 AA/Anna Mockford and Nick Bonetti; 31 AA/Simon McBride; 32 Alamy/Eye Ubiquitous; 33 Alamy/Martin Norris; 34/35 4Corners/Amantini Stefano; 36 AA/Dario Miterdiri; 37 Sarah Quill/Alamy; 39 AA/Anna Mockford and Nick Bonetti; 40 Atlantide Phototravel/Corbis ; 43 4Corners/SIME/Johanna Huber; 45 Alamy/avatra images; 46 4Corners/SIME/Baviera Guido; 48/49 photolibrary.com/Hemis; 50 AA/Simon McBride; 51 photolibrary.com/Mauritius ; 53 photolibrary.com/Rafael Macia; 54 Melvyn Longhurst/Alamy; 56 4Corners/SIME/Carassale Ferruccio; 58 AA/Anna Mockford and Nick Bonetti; 61 AA/Anna Mockford and Nick Bonetti; 62/63 photolibrary.com/Jon Arnold Travel; 64 AA/Anna Mockford and Nick Bonetti; 67 AA/Anna Mockford and Nick Bonetti; 68 AA/Anna Mockford and Nick Bonetti; 69 AA/Clive Sawyer; 70 AA/Anna Mockford and Nick Bonetti; 73 AA/Dario Miterdiri; 75 AA/Anna Mockford and Nick Bonetti; 76/77 AA/Anna Mockford and Nick Bonetti; 78 AA/Anna Mockford and Nick Bonetti; 81 AA/Anna Mockford and Nick Bonetti; 83 AA/Anna Mockford and Nick Bonetti; 84 4Corners/SIME/Kaos02; 87 photolibrary.com/De Agostini Editore; 88 AA/Anna Mockford and Nick Bonetti; 90/91 SuperStock/age fotostock; 92 AA/Dario Miterdiri; 95 4Corners/SIME/Johanna Huber; 97 AA/Anna Mockford and Nick Bonetti; 98 SuperStock/age fotostock; 99 AA/Anna Mockford and Nick Bonetti; 101 Glenn Harper/Alamy; 102/103 AA/Anna Mockford and Nick Bonetti; 104/105 Getty/Christian Kober; 106 AA/Clive Sawyer; 107 Alamy/Paul Carstairs; 109 4Corners/Amantini Stefano; 110 Alamy/Massimo Pizzotti; 112 AA/Anna Mockford and Nick Bonetti; 113 "Corbis/Marco Cristofori"; 115 AA/Clive Sawyer; 116 AA/Anna Mockford and Nick Bonetti; 118/119 AA/Anna Mockford and Nick Bonetti; 120 4Corners/Borchi Massimo; 123 AA/Simon McBride; 125 Alamy/Worldwide Picture Library; 126 Alamy/Sarah Quill; 127 AA/Clive Sawyer; 129 The Bridgeman Art Library/Cameraphoto Arte Venezia; 130 Alamy/Sarah Quill; 132/133 Alamy/Peter Barritt; 134 imagebroker/Alamy; 135 AA/Anna Mockford and Nick Bonetti; 137 Alamy/Chuck Pefley; 138 Dorling Kindersley/Demetrio Carrasco ; 140 Alamy/Barry Mason; 143 AA/Simon McBride; 144 AA/Anna Mockford and Nick Bonetti; 146/147 AA/Simon McBride; 148 AA/Anna Mockford and Nick Bonetti; 151 Dennis Jones/Lonely Planet; 152/153 photolibrary.com/Robert Harding Travel; 154 AA/Dario Miterdiri; 155 AA/Anna Mockford and Nick Bonetti; 157 AA/Anna Mockford and Nick Bonetti; 158 AA/Anna Mockford and Nick Bonetti; 160/161 AA/Dario Miterdiri; 162 Nic Cleave Photography/Alamy; 163 AA/Anna Mockford and Nick Bonetti; 165 AA/Simon McBride; 167 Sarah Quill/Alamy; 168 AA/Anna Mockford and Nick Bonetti; 171 AA/Anna Mockford and Nick Bonetti; 172 Alamy/Zbigniew Tomaszewski; 173 Paul Carstairs/Alamy.   Every effort has been made to trace copyright holders. We apologize in advance for any unintentional omissions or errors and would be pleased to apply any corrections in following editions of this publication..